THE COIN COLLECTOR'S FACT BOOK

BY WALTER J. ZIMMERMAN

ARCO

New York

Published by Arco Publishing Company, Inc.
219 Park Avenue South, New York, N.Y. 10003

Copyright © 1974 by Walter J. Zimmerman

Library of Congress Catalog Card Number 73-77839

ISBN 0-668-02991-9

Printed in the United States of America

To Verena

ACKNOWLEDGMENTS

For aid in making available a great many photographs of coins used in this book, the author wishes to express his appreciation to the American Numismatic Society and Mrs. Beulah P. Shonnard in particular. Also to Mr. Douglas G. Liddell of Spink & Son Ltd., London, for his kindness in procuring other illustrations from the British Museum collection. As always, Messrs. Henry Grunthal and Hillel Kaslove of the A.N.S. were most helpful with their knowledge and time.

Contents

Introduction 1

How and What Coin Collectors Collect 3

Specialization 5

Fake Coins Made to Deceive Collectors 8

Selected List of Books and Periodicals 9

Associations, Clubs and Collections Open to
the Public 12

Finding a Valuable Coin in Change 14

What Is a Rare Coin? 16

How to Collect—by Type or Date 18

Coin Collecting—Hobby or Investment Opportunity 19

Grading or Condition of Coins 21

How to Handle and Preserve Your Coins 26

Displaying Your Collection 33

Really Old Coins Still Available to Collectors 35

The Beginnings of Coinage 37

Coining Techniques—Ancient, Medieval, and Modern 41

Coins of the Romans and the Byzantines 48

Medieval and Renaissance Coins 52

Dollar-Sized Silver Coins 56

Die Engraving, Errors, and Resulting Varieties 59

Early Coins of Colonial America 62

Mints of the United States 66

Coin Types of the United States 68

Long Discontinued Denominations 80

U.S. Gold Coins 84

Privately Minted Gold Pieces 90

Commemorative Coins 93

U.S. Proof and Special Mint Coins 97

Foreign Coins That Were Once Legal Tender in
the U.S. 99

Siege Pieces, Money of Necessity, Countermarked,
and Overstruck Coins 103

Primitive, Commodity, and Curious Money 106

Tokens 109

Paper Money 116

Medals 124

A Short Glossary of Numismatic Terms 130

Introduction

So you have decided to collect coins! What prompted you to do so? Is it the history or the economics represented in those stamped pieces of metal that first appealed to you? Perhaps the beauty of their design and craftsmanship fascinates you, for coins are really examples in miniature of the sculptor's and die engraver's arts. Or perhaps you were given a handful of interesting-looking coins and you want to learn more about them—if only to know what they are worth.

Regardless of your reasons for collecting, you are in good company. You now share a common interest with quite a segment of the world's people. Several million Americans collect coins in some fashion and this hobby is also entrenched in just about all of the other countries of the globe. Age group? Well, anywhere from six years old to over 90, and the women among them are usually just as knowledgeable as the men.

It is fun to collect coins. More than that, you will find doing so can be very rewarding. In fact, when taken seriously the hobby has a way of broadening one's outlook. If you do reach the point of becoming a serious student of coins and coinage you might prefer to call yourself a *numismatist* and your hobby *numismatics*. That's from the Latin *numisma* meaning "coin" and is now applied to the science of coins and such related items as medals, tokens, and paper money.

The nice part is that the enjoyment and educational value of numismatics can be obtained at a cost that doesn't require too much more than ordinary spending money—provided you promise to forego a search for rarities which are, naturally, always expensive.

It will be the purpose of this book to give the reader a number of pointers about coins and coin collecting which will help him to get pleasure from his hobby while also making him wary of the traps of the collecting urge and the tendency to lose one's reason (temporarily, at least). Then he can take off in whatever direction his interest may lead.

Sketched briefly on these pages will also be the story of the U.S. coins as well as those in history that preceded and influenced them. But bear in mind that for a full background one would require at least several dictionary-sized books each for ancient Greece, Rome and their dependencies, and tomes just as weighty for the nations that followed.

Then there is the coinage of the modern world, of which the inquiring-minded collector should have a working knowledge.

In any event, if this book can at least whet your numismatic appetite, it will have accomplished its mission. It makes no claim to being a complete guide to anything and the author hopes it will not be so construed.

Except in a few instances, all coins reproduced throughout this book are actual size. However, when you begin to examine your coins critically (and those you may wish to acquire) a good magnifying glass is very helpful in order to bring up minute details and, possibly, imperfections which the naked eye will overlook. Collectors usually prefer at least a six-power (6x) glass for the purpose and frequently carry it with them wherever they go. The coins illustrated on this page are twice actual size. Even though they are fine specimens the enlargement shows more clearly the points of wear as well as small nicks and scratches.

How and What Coin Collectors Collect

Most beginners are date collectors. They start by collecting the coins of their own country by denomination, date, and place of minting. They may purchase standard folders with holes punched into them such as those designed to fit the popular U.S. Lincoln cents, first issued in 1909. Each day they examine the cents they receive in change, or bother their family and friends for a look at theirs. Gradually, many of the blank spaces are filled, particularly for the most recent dates.

Pretty soon the collector will discover how practically impossible it is to obtain the other dates and mint marks from circulation. This is the period that distinguishes the real coin enthusiast from the rank and file.

Of course, sometimes the older pieces will turn up, but, when they do, you can be sure their condition will be quite poor. Unless they happen to be the rare ones, they'll have little numismatic appeal and, besides, be worth exactly their face value. Here is where the "grading" or condition of the coin enters the picture as a very important factor.

If you are really determined to fill that book, a coin dealer can usually supply much of what is missing at prices ranging from very little to very much, depending upon the degree of rarity and the condition of the coin you may purchase.

Reliable dealers can be found in most cities across the country and it is worthwhile to get to know some of them. Besides supplying you with coins, they can also be sources of numismatic information not otherwise easily obtainable.

Some dealers issue "fixed price" catalogs listing the coins they have for sale. Thus you can order your wants through the mail if it is inconvenient to get to the shop. Naturally, you must expect them to make a profit on what they sell, even though what you may buy happens to be a coin of familiar appearance which seems to be no different from all the others in the series—and thus, to the uninitiated, ought not be worth more than face value. For example, the Lincoln

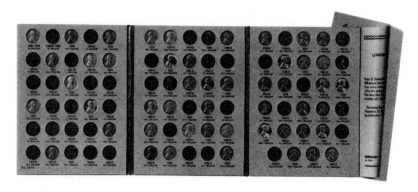

Beginning coin collectors usually start like this.
(Photo courtesy of Whitman Coin Products.)

cent of 1909 "S-VDB" (San Francisco mint with the initials of the designer, Victor D. Brenner) is rare and, in uncirculated condition, has brought about $200 at recent auctions. Yet basically it looks like others you got as change today.

There are other ways to obtain coins, although having a collector for a father or grandfather is still unbeatable. You might try swapping with your friends, including those who attend the local coin club (you should join one).

Also, there are auctions. Coin auctions are really what set the values. Sometimes you may be able to attend them personally, but it is also possible to send in mail bids from the auction catalogs.

A number of firms that conduct periodic auctions offer subscriptions to their sale catalogs as issued, and soon afterwards will supply listings of "prices realized" for each lot therein. By comparing the sale prices with your own bid (or what might have been your bid if you'd chanced one), you will gradually learn what the coins you are interested in are worth on the market.

Many of the catalogs include a series of "plates" or pages of illustrations to show the appearance and condition of specific items. Along with the terse descriptive matter accompanying each lot, there will often be an estimate of what the auction house thinks it may bring at the sale. Of course, you are under no obligation to bid at that price. Many times a coin estimated at, say, $25 will actually go for considerably less. But it could just as well end up being more if the piece is of great interest and the bidding is unusually keen.

Specialization

Usually, a collector will specialize in the coinage of a single country if it is not overly extensive. Otherwise, he will concentrate on a section of it. The reason is that the field of numismatics is too vast for a single collector to cope with everything. What you will do, no doubt, is decide for yourself which area or areas of specialization interest you. As you go along, you are bound to find some fascinating, while others may leave you cold.

One of the least expensive and still most gratifying spheres for the beginner (and for advanced collectors, too) is the coinage of the modern world. As this implies, you would be on the lookout for examples of current coins from all over the globe. This might even be the best way to get started, because in collecting modern coins you may hit upon a country or several of them in which you will have a strong urge to specialize. For example, the coins of the new nations of Africa are now being sought with great interest and many collectors have become quite knowledgeable about them. They are generally not expensive. Because so many of these nations have issued coins for no more than about 25 years, you can really start on the ground floor.

If you travel abroad or know people who do, see that you get sets of the coinage of the countries visited. You might try to convey to your friends who promise to bring them back for you that you'd like all pieces in uncirculated condition wherever possible. There are coin dealers in all the major cities where your friends can get them, or perhaps they might not mind stopping in at a bank when in a foreign city. Tellers there are often cooperative in selecting freshly minted coins from the change drawers and do so without premium. Remember that worn pieces, particularly of modern world coins, have little or no numismatic value.

Within recent years the mints of various countries, or their appointed agents, have cooperated with collectors to the extent that they will supply proof sets or uncirculated sets of their new issues, usually in special mounts, at established prices.

5

Many collectors find satisfaction in collecting the coins of England, Canada, and the other Commonwealth countries and dependencies. This is logical as well as highly interesting since we share a common language and heritage. And, of course, the coins of England were circulated here during colonial days and for quite some time after.

Of course, below our southwestern border we have a great neighbor whose coinage antedates ours by over a few hundred years. Mexican coins, both minted under the Spanish monarchy and since, offer an interesting challenge to many collectors because of the wide variety of types available—and the history built into them.

There are many other kinds of numismatic specialization. One is collecting by size, the most popular being the dollar-sized coins. Another is collecting by subject. If you like ships, or architecture, you may want to gather together a collection of coins that feature them. These motifs, by the way, have appeared on coins from ancient times. Some concentrate solely on the eagle, the favored bird of coinage because of its heraldic symbolism through the ages. Animals are also popular, particularly the lion, and many collectors prefer not to limit their "zoos," taking on not only all beasts they can find but everything that flies, too.

You might decide to collect coins with religious motifs or significance. Not only have Christ, the Madonna, and many saints appeared throughout the history of coinage but religious mottos and legends have also been prevalent. "In God We Trust" is the U.S. contribution to this—since 1864, in fact, when it was included on the new two cent pieces.

The list of such subjects is practically endless. It is safe to say that, if you wish to take advantage of this approach to numismatics, you will find many examples of your immediate specialty both in modern and ancient coinages. It will also give you the opportunity to broaden your base, i.e., you will be cutting across national boundaries and many centuries. Birds, for example, are portrayed on ancient Greek and Roman coins as well as on those of modern England, Canada, Eire, and many other nations. And don't forget the eagle on the current U.S. coinage.

A single moment in world history can become an interesting numismatic experience. There are those who specialize in the Napoleonic period, the times during or right after World Wars I and II, or almost any other time in history that interests them.

Modern "coins of the world" are usually considered to range from about 1850 to the present. As always, though, many of the older pieces and some of comparatively recent date, such as a few shown here, have become rarities. Here is a sampling of typical nineteenth and twentieth century coins including a handful from Mexico and Canada.

Fake Coins Made to Deceive Collectors

Today it is an extremely rare experience to find counterfeit coins in change. (Paper money is something else again.) Apparently, it is no longer feasible or financially worthwhile for counterfeiters to produce and distribute run-of-the-mill quarters and dimes, for example.

But counterfeiters are still active in another sphere and their victims are collectors. They have simply transferred their skills to the specialized field of supplying excellent forgeries of many kinds of rare coins to the unwary. These fakes are often extremely well executed and can easily deceive the average collector—and quite often dealers, too. Ordinary counterfeits of silver coins used to be mostly of lead. The new fakes for collectors, however, are always of pure silver, sometimes even finer in quality than the genuine coin. The counterfeiters can afford this easily, of course, because they ask premium rates for the fake "rare coins" they issue. The desire of collectors to have rare gold and copper coins, as well as silver, ancient and modern, is grist to their mill.

Besides the out-and-out fakes, certain real coins are sometimes reworked to change date or mint mark in order to make them numismatically more valuable.

Not to be overlooked while we touch on counterfeits is the large array of copies of many old coins supplied for use in large quantity as advertising promotions. Usually, these are cast from an original piece without criminal intent at all. Unfortunately, however, some of them have been sold as originals by unscrupulous dealers to those who simply don't know anything about coins but feel they would like to have a few old ones at a bargain.

So, when someone you never heard of offers to sell you rare coins at bargain prices, don't snap them up until you learn more about him.

Selected List of Books
and Periodicals

Books

It has been said, "Get the book first; then buy the coin." This is sound advice. Intensive reading about the coins you wish to collect will gradually build up a solid background in your specialty. You may even become an expert in it yourself. Books are available on numismatic material of all kinds from modern world coinage to ancient Greek and Roman and all points between. Others will tell you about paper money or medals or tokens.

Some of these books are written to give the reader a broad panorama but most concentrate on a single country or specialized phase of numismatics. Just to name two highly specialized books, there is Dr. Sheldon's *Penny Whimsey* which discusses and illustrates the early series of U.S. large cents, including its many varieties which are legion. Another is *The Fantastic 1804 Dollar* (Newman/Bressett) on the rarest of all U.S. coins. The authors have done much painstaking research on it.

A great many books are basically catalogs with brief descriptions of each series, listings of the dates of coining, and illustrations of the pieces. They will also include the current estimated market value (what the collector might have to pay—not what he would receive). One of these is the *Guide Book of United States Coins*, usually called the "Red Book" and, for the collector, the most indispensable of its kind. Available at a nominal price and published every year, it includes every type of U.S. coin ever struck, along with Colonial coins and token currency. Current retail valuations for the various grades of condition as well as other information of importance is provided.

Below, you will find a small list of books which a knowledgeable collector might like to have as a nucleus for his personal numismatic library.

Brooke: *English Coins.* (Discusses English coinage from earliest times.)
Brown and Dunn: *Grading U.S. Coins.*
Buttrey and Hubbord: *A Guide Book of Mexican Coins.*
Carson: *Coins of the World.* (A general survey from earliest times.)
Charlton: *Standard Catalog of Canadian Coins, Tokens and Paper Money* (1973).
Craig: *Coins of the World, 1750–1850.* (A catalog.)
Davenport: *European Crowns and Talers 1700–1800.* (A catalog.)
Davenport: *European Crowns and Talers Since 1800.* (A catalog.)
Dowle and Finn: *Guidebook to the Coinage of Ireland.*
Friedberg: *Gold Coins of the World* (3rd edition).
Friedberg: *Paper Money of the U.S.*
Goodacre: *A Handbook of the Coins of the Byzantine Empire.* (History and listings.)
Krause and Mishler: *Standard Catalog of World Coins.*
Mattingly: *Roman Coins.* (The ancient Roman Republic and Empire.)
Newman: *The Early Paper Money of America.*
Schilke and Solomon: *America's Foreign Coins.* (Describes foreign coins current in U.S. to 1857.)
Seaby: *Greek Coins and Their Values.*
Seaby: *Roman Coins and Their Values.*
Seaby: *Standard Catalog of English Coins.*
Seltman: *Greek Coins.* (A history of the ancient Greek coinage.)
Stewart: *The Scottish Coinage.*
Yeoman: *A Guide Book of United States Coins (The Red Book).* Published annually.

Periodicals

There are a number of worthy magazines available to keep you abreast of developments in the world of numismatics. They contain articles on various aspects of coins and coinage as well as news of coin conventions, clubs, personalities in the field, reviews of new books, and so on. Also, many dealers advertise material for sale in these magazines. Such listings reflect the market prices of a good cross-section of the coins you might want for your own collection, or at least want to know something about.

The magazines will also give you an excellent idea of what is being collected actively, which has a great bearing on the prices you will have to pay.

Many newspapers throughout the country carry a column or two on coin matters at least once a week, as for example, *The New York Times* on Sundays.

The names and addresses of some of the periodicals issued in the U.S., Canada, and England are listed here, for they are seldom found on newsstands. You will notice that a few of them, published by dealers, also include fixed price lists along with their editorial material. The magazines are issued anywhere from weekly to quarterly. You may wish to write one or two of them for sample copies.

Canadian Numismatic Journal. Published by Canadian Numismatic Association, Willowdale, Ontario, Canada.

Coinage. Encino, California.

Coins. Iola, Wisconsin.

Coin World. Sidney, Ohio.

Medal Collector. Fort Montgomery, New York. (Official publication of the Orders and Medals Society of America.)

Numismatic Circular. Published by Spink & Son, Ltd., 5 King Street, St. James's, London SW1, England. Includes fixed price list.

Numismatic News Weekly. Iola, Wisconsin.

Numismatic Review (and Coin Galleries Fixed Price List). Published by Coin Galleries, 123 West 57th Street, New York, N.Y. 10019.

The Numismatist. P. O. Box 2366, Colorado Springs, Colo. 80801. (Official publication of The American Numismatic Association.)

Paper Money. Jefferson, Wisconsin. (Official publication of the Society of Paper Money Collectors.)

Seaby's Coin & Medal Bulletin. Published by B. A. Seaby, Ltd., Audley House, 11 Margaret Street, Oxford Circus, London, W1 BAT, England. Includes fixed price list.

TAMS Journal. Sepulveda, California. (The official organ of the Token & Medal Society.)

World Coins. Sidney, Ohio.

Whitman Numismatic Journal. Racine, Wisconsin.

Associations, Clubs, and Collections Open to the Public

American Numismatic Association: Every coin collector should become a member of this national educational organization which was founded in 1891 to further interest in all things numismatic. There is a small non-recurring initiation fee for the first year and the yearly dues are eight dollars, which also entitles you to the association's excellent monthly magazine, *The Numismatist.* Its membership is also open to juniors 12 years old and over. The A.N.A. has an extensive library and collection of numismatic material at its headquarters building. A national convention is held each year in a different city and draws members from all over the country. There are collections of all kinds on display, lectures, and "Bourse" tables—i.e., dealers bring their available material for sale—as well as an auction. You can write to the A.N.A. at 818 North Cascade Blvd., Colorado Springs, Colo. 80901 for further details.

The American Numismatic Society: 155th and 156th Streets & Broadway, New York, N.Y. 10032. The Society, founded in 1865, is a more scholarly organization. Its museum houses a tremendous collection of coins and related items and probably the largest library of its kind in the United States, featuring material on ancient, medieval, and modern subjects. You can become an associate member for $15 a year, which entitles you to receive its occasional publications, mostly on the technical aspects of ancient and medieval coins. Lectures are held in conjunction with the Society's quarterly meetings to which members and the general public are invited. The museum is open six days a week.

Clubs: The local coin club is the ideal place to meet others with numismatic interests and exchange ideas, or listen to what they have to say. If you do not as yet know what clubs are active in your vicinity, write to the American Numismatic Association and they will no doubt give you a list of those nearest you. Lasting friendships are frequently made at these special interest clubs. Meetings are usually held monthly and, as a rule, dues are nominal.

Collections Open to the Public: While most museums, colleges, and banks do not usually have permanent collections, many of them will at least have an occasional loan exhibit on some branch of numismatics.

Permanent collections may be seen at the museum of the American Numismatic Society, the American Numismatic Association (both mentioned earlier), and the national collection housed at the Smithsonian Institution in Washington, D.C. Besides these, the following are well worth visiting: The Chase Manhattan Bank's Money Museum (New York); the collection of The National Bank of Detroit; The Federal Reserve Bank (Philadelphia); The Ford Museum (Dearborn, Michigan); The Omaha Public Library; The Newport Balboa Savings & Loan Association (Newport Beach, California, near Los Angeles).

Coin clubs and regional associations will from time to time during the year sponsor conventions where an important feature will be exhibits of members' material. Up to a point, dealers will be willing to allow serious collectors to browse at their bourse tables there, or in their own display rooms, although they are naturally in business to make sales.

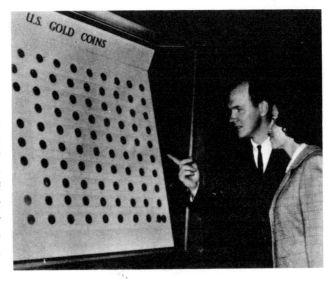

One of the 19 specially designed cases displaying coins at the Smithsonian Institution's Hall of Monetary History and Medallic Art which opened to the public in October, 1964.

Finding a Valuable Coin
in Change?

Unfortunately, it is no longer possible to find much else but the current coins still circulating. This is particularly so now that the present market value of the silver in the 1964 and earlier pieces exceeds their face value. The very old pieces such as the Indian head cents and Liberty and Buffalo nickels have long since disappeared.

Frankly, the chances of finding anything of value in the change you receive are not good and they grow smaller and smaller as the days go by. This is written soberly, with proper cognizance of the many advertisements whose headlines proclaim that you may have a fortune in rare coins in your pocket right now if you will only examine them.

This is not to say it *can't* happen to you, but one should be realistic. Bank tellers, merchants, even bus drivers, all of whom have access to coins in quantity—and don't forget the host of collectors and dealers—have for years been examining the money that passes through their hands, culling what they think might have numismatic value.

It is true that over ten years ago this writer did find an 1853 quarter dollar in his pocket one evening, condition about "Fine" and thus worth then a couple of dollars (possibly more now). Then there was that uncirculated Stone Mountain commemorative half dollar also obtained in change, and perhaps of equal value. You might say that these two "finds" are about par for the course—or above par.

It is really easier to come across valuable pieces in a safe deposit box left by one's grandfather than to turn up anything numismatically important by chance at the end of the day. But who knows? You may be one of the lucky few.

Numismatics has plenty to offer the collector in that it is a mighty interesting and stimulating hobby which does not have to depend upon windfalls. Expect to obtain your finds the way other collectors do—through dealers and auctions and possibly by swapping. Then you won't be disappointed.

A final comment on the subject is the story this writer read as a lad which told of a man who found a five dollar gold piece that lay in the street. He never saw the sun again because as he walked, his eyes were henceforth glued to the pavement in the hope of finding another bonanza.

What Is a Rare Coin?

You will quickly learn which dates and mint marks in the U.S. series are the rare ones. Just look at the "Red Book" and compare the prices at which they are cataloged. The basis for rarity is established from the mint records which show how many were actually struck. On the other hand, when coins become badly worn, they are constantly taken out of circulation by the banks and returned to the mint where they are melted down for their metal, to be recoined later in the current types. Of course, the collections of numismatists and dealers' stocks account for the unavailability of many more pieces.

Thus, even though many millions of a particular coin may have been struck in the year of issue, attrition of one kind or another reduces the quantity available to the collector. This is particularly the case when you look for the better grades.

There are some coin series that simply do not interest collectors as much as others, nor are all really old pieces necessarily expensive in relation to more recent ones. For example, if you are not fussy about having the important "key" dates, you can still buy early half dollars or large cents in collectible condition for no more than what certain twentieth century key date dimes might cost. And there are many ancient coins, 2,000 years or more old (Roman and others), which you can obtain in reasonable condition for a handful of dollars each. Certainly these old coins are "rare" if only because of their antiquity.

Not so many years ago U.S. silver dollars from 1878 on were not a popular series and often could be obtained at banks as currency at face value in uncirculated condition. These large "cartwheels," as they were called, rarely circulated except in the far West, with the result that they were returned to the banks to be exchanged for paper currency. So even though they were almost 100 years old the denomination was unwanted, except by a handful of collectors who looked for rare dates and mint marks. Later the silver dollar became more popular with collectors and the price went up on the better pieces. This was at a time long before it was thought there would be a possibility of our government reducing the silver content of our coins—or removing it entirely, as finally happened to be the case. Now any silver dollar, regardless of condition, commands a premium.

Brasher Doubloon, 1787; it is excessively rare. You'll never find this.

How to Collect — by Type or Date?

Collecting a series of coins by date gets harder and harder and more expensive as you go along. You will not only have the dates to worry about but also the mint marks. Going back to your Lincoln cent collection, you will notice that three holes are generally provided in the folder you wish to fill for every date through 1955 (except in certain years). After that, you will find only two for a while. The holes are for coins struck each year at the Philadelphia, Denver, and San Francisco mints. In 1956, the operation of the San Francisco mint was discontinued for general purposes but was resumed again in 1968.

It is quite difficult (although a little easier if one lives on the west coast) to find suitable pieces in change struck at the San Francisco (S) mint. By now most of the older ones seem to have been culled from circulation and those more recently issued have had comparatively small mintings. The Denver (D) and Philadelphia minted coins (the latter without mint mark at all except on one small run of five cent pieces) are easier to come by. But in any event, what do you have when you do get as many coins as possible lined up, with or without the aid of a dealer? *Coins all looking essentially alike, except for date.*

One suggestion is to fill the books as well as you are able, but when you get bogged down, don't give up numismatics. Think along the lines of a "type" collection of U.S. coins as a starter. "Type" refers to the various series of coins within a denomination, most of which have had periodic design changes. Try to have one or a few examples of each in as many different denominations as possible, and in as fine condition as you can afford. Some collectors try for the first and last dates of a given type, but this is not essential. In any event, your collection will take on a more interesting, fresher look if you plan it around type lines rather than date.

Coin Collecting — Hobby or Investment Opportunity?

The serious collector will consider coins something to study, exhibit, and add to as he expands his interests (and no doubt, his pocketbook). However, the value of rare coins—and those that may become rare as time goes on—has risen steadily with the years and there is no reason to believe the trend will not continue. New collectors constantly enter the market and, in effect, bid against each other for the limited amount of available material.

If your selections are made with proper care and insight, you should reasonably expect that some years hence, if you decide to sell all or part of your collection, you will get more than you paid for it. This gives you the opportunity to "have your cake and eat it too." It really is pleasant to know that one can enjoy a hobby for as long as he wishes and then end up by realizing as much as or more than he put into it.

Rare coins, then, always have a market. But when and if you are ready to sell your collection, don't be disappointed if many of the pieces in it just don't rate an offer from the dealers to whom you submit them. It may be that these dealers are overstocked on the particular items, or the condition is unsatisfactory for their trade. Then again, many dealers are specialists themselves and some do not have a market for certain series whereas others might. Sometimes, too, what you thought was rare and valuable just happens not to be.

As in the disposal of any merchandise or commodity (and coins enter this category when they have numismatic interest), it is necessary to bring the right buyer together with the seller. And, of course, a dealer who buys from you must eventually sell to someone else at a profit. If he doesn't think he can, there will be no deal.

There are wealthy people with large amounts of cash to invest who have no interest at all in the numismatic aspect of collecting.

19

Nonetheless they buy up rare coins expecting them to appreciate in value. If done properly, this practice will eventually pay off, sometimes handsomely—particularly when the right guidance is obtained and followed. You may also have heard of the other "collectors" (actually speculators) who stockpile as many as hundreds of rolls of shiny new cents, nickels, dimes, quarters, and halves in the year of issue, hoping to be able to sell them years later to beginning collectors at a considerable profit.

A handful of these people might do well by themselves in the long run at the expense of the real collector, but, more often than not, they would have done better by opening an account in a savings bank.

The collector with numismatic fervor takes his pleasure from studying coins regardless of what they might be worth at any given moment. The price fluctuations in the marketplace, while interesting to be sure, should not be all-important.

Grading or Condition of Coins

The Importance of Condition to Their Numismatic Value

Most coins are issued for use as a medium of exchange and, therefore, they are expected to be handled constantly. Perhaps in a month or so, 50 or more people will have handled the change now in your pocket or handbag. So, very quickly a coin loses its mint lustre and begins to wear down from abrasion during constant circulation. First to go are the high points of the design. Then the wear spreads to other areas. Usually the detail of the obverse disappears before that of the reverse. Sometimes with long wear the lettering and the date will become difficult to read or be partly or completely obliterated.

Numismatists have a formula to describe the condition of a coin, i.e., the degree of preservation. This grading, as it is called, is listed below:

UNC:	Brilliant uncirculated or perfect mint state. Also known in Europe as "FDC"—Fleur de coin.
EF:	Extremely fine. Almost but not absolutely perfect.
VF:	Very fine. Slight wear on the high spots.
F:	Fine. The coin is worn but the design is still quite distinct although flat.
G:	Good. Considerably worn, but all features are discernible and the date can be read easily.
Fair:	Extremely worn, but the design and lettering may be identified.
M or P:	Mediocre or Poor. An inferior piece with the features indistinct.

Proof coins will be dealt with later.

Between two ascending or descending grades, even an expert sometimes finds it difficult to place the exact condition of a coin. Occasionally, you will see that a coin is graded VF–EF or V–VF, for example. In the first instance, the dash will indicate that the grade is better than Very Fine but not quite Extremely Fine. In the second example, it is somewhere between Fine and Very Fine. Some numismatists vary the nomenclature by qualifying the condition of a coin as, for example, "Good EF" (better than EF) or "Nearly EF" (not quite EF).

As mentioned earlier, in most instances coins do not wear evenly on both sides. Thus, a coin's grading might be described as F/VF, or EF/VF. The condition before the slash mark would apply to the obverse and the one after it to the reverse.

You can see from all this that while coin grading has been treated with great care, it is still not an exact science and apparently never will be. So, if the professionals have difficulty in grading borderline coins with absolute certainty, it is bound to be even more difficult for the beginning collector.

Dealers of repute pride themselves on describing very fairly the condition of the coins they have for sale. But it has been said jokingly that when one wants to sell he upgrades the coin, while the buyer will downgrade it—until he owns it! It is simply human nature to do this. Remember that when one buys or sells, coins being no exception, the requirements include mutual trust, knowledge, and a degree of watchfulness.

In any event, as you examine or buy actual coins, you will gradually develop a sixth sense as to their rank in the grading table and, thus, to the price you will have to pay. If you become friendly with a dealer, he will no doubt gladly show you the gradations of condition of a coin series, as far as he is able, from his stock.

Below you will find illustrations of typical grading for a single coin type, but to make it stick you will need to see the coins themselves. We might mention that different coin types, because of their unique designs, do not wear the same.

In many instances the quality of the "strike" at the mint will have a great deal to do with the condition of a coin. Remember that millions of pieces go through the coining presses daily. For one reason or another some coins may have been struck more weakly than others. Someday you may see two uncirculated pieces of the same denomination, date and mint mark, of which one is sharply defined in all its features. The other by comparison will leave much to be desired and consequently will be worth considerably less numismatically.

Even perfect coins can become marred between the time they leave the mint and they reach circulation. They may show nicks or scratches, the result of "bagging" and later stacking and general handling at the bank.

The Importance of Condition

Extremely fine or uncirculated coins, even those which under no circumstances might be considered rare, command a considerably higher price than those in the lower grades. For example, a dime which may be purchased from a dealer as "Good" for 50 cents and in EF condition for five dollars or so may perhaps jump in uncirculated state to $20 or more, especially if the mint lustre is intact or the piece has developed attractive toning. Knowing this, the discriminating collector will try, where possible, to acquire his coins in the top grades, except when he is looking for rare pieces. In such cases, he may not be able to afford their high prices. From time to time it is, at best, impossible to obtain certain rarities in other than so-so condition.

GRADING THE JEFFERSON NICKEL

Uncirculated   (Unc)

Extremely Fine   (EF)

The cheekbone, eyebrow, and hairlines only slightly worn.
Portico pillars at reverse below the dome will be weak.

Fine   (F)

Cheekbone flat; eyebrow and hairline rather worn.
Collar line faint and pillars at reverse are weak.

Very Good (VG)

Jefferson's collar shows considerable wear. Pillars almost gone.

Good (G)

Considerably worn overall; bottom line of collar above left shoulder has disappeared; lettering has become flat but readable.

How to Handle and Preserve Your Coins

Always hold a coin at the edges between your thumb and forefinger, if you have to handle it at all. Never hold it any other way. The reason is that the chemicals in your fingers can cause a reaction in the metal of the coin, possibly starting an unpleasant stain or tarnish over the piece. Metals also react badly to various common substances. A rubber band carelessly dropped on a silver piece will leave a black mark virtually impossible to remove.

Also, make sure that the 2″ x 2″ paper envelopes you may use to store your coins are sulphur-free (most of them are) because sulphuric acid, used in making many papers, will cause oxidization. Do not keep copper and silver coins together in the same box, even while they are in envelopes, because one metal may have a reaction to the other.

Whatever you do, make sure never to jumble your coins together loose in a box. They will become scratched and automatically deteriorate in appearance and value. Rare coins handled by careless or inexperienced collectors have unintentionally been downgraded from the condition in which they were obtained.

Silver coins fresh from the mint have a bright lustre which gradually softens and disappears after a short time in circulation. However, some uncirculated silver coins held by collectors "tone," developing an attractive iridescent coloring (blue, green, or red, for example). If anything, this adds to their beauty and value. Copper or bronze coins sometimes turn a handsome red or chocolate brown.

Ancient and medieval coins, many of which are dug out of the earth having been buried there for century upon century, are often found to have a completely green patina. This is due to the acids in the soil causing a reaction in the coin.

Most natural tonings and patinas are pleasing and under no circumstance should they be removed by attempts at cleaning. Without this "weathering" effect, what you would have left might be a lifeless piece of metal. Generally speaking, never clean your coins, even though you may have some silver pieces that are oxidized completely black, which happens occasionally.

It is suggested that you ignore the many chemical preparations sold for cleaning purposes because they seldom help and sometimes, in fact, can do irreparable damage. To remove surface dirt, however, you might try a paste of ordinary baking soda and water. Nothing else should be used.

Coins brought up from the sea or earth are often so heavily encrusted with verdigris or other matter that they are unrecognizable, and experts do have a way of cleaning them. It is doubtful that you would ever obtain coins first-hand in such weathered condition, but if by chance you happen to come across such a find, for once *don't* try to "do it yourself."

Storing Your Coins

The 2″ x 2″ paper envelope has already been mentioned. This is as convenient as any method because you can write the description of the coin you've placed inside it directly on the envelope itself, either in ink or with a typewriter. It has the added advantage of being the least expensive method of storage. Some go a step further by slipping the coin first in a small glassine or acetate envelope for extra protection against handling and possible abrasion.

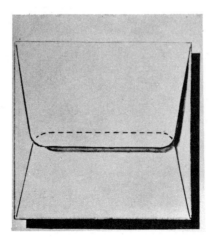

The 2″ x 2″ opaque paper envelope; you can write on it as you like.

Envelopes can also be obtained in heavier plastics, although these have always seemed unnecessary to this writer. Nor can they be written on. The paper envelope, costing less and having the least bulk, will generally fit any coin you happen to own, from the tiniest to slightly larger than dollar size.

There are variations on this theme. One is to buy cardboards prepared with diecut holes covered with acetate, which fold over to 2″ x 2″. The collector slips the coin inside and staples the open sides together. Any description is written directly on the cardboard. This method eliminates excess handling of the coins and gives excellent visibility, something paper envelopes cannot offer.

What do you do when the quantity of small coin-filled envelopes of one type or another mounts to inconvenient proportions? You can obtain cardboard, metal, plastic, or wooden (never oak) boxes that will hold anywhere from 100 to 200 coins or more depending upon thickness.

Coin storage box (plastic) for 2″ x 2″ envelopes and coin holders. (Photo courtesy of Whitman Coin Products.)

We have discussed the coin books. They can be purchased for all denominations of U.S., Canadian, and modern English coins, with or without descriptive printing. Their cost depends upon their elaborateness. The ordinary three- or four-fold variety whose holes are not covered with acetate is quite inexpensive.

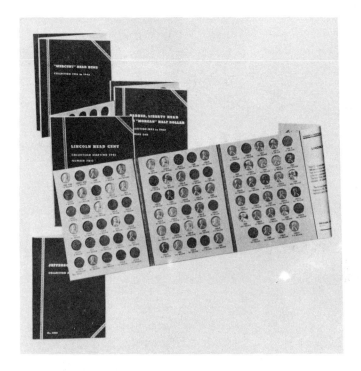

If you become a date collector you can find many types of folders and albums at various prices for all U.S., Canadian, and British coin series. This one is quite practical and inexpensive. (Photo courtesy of Whitman Coin Products.)

Some collectors mount their coins in rigid lucite holders of varying size. Others prefer trays, compartmented or not, which in turn will fit into a cabinet, frequently of cloth or plastic covered cardboard, which may do double duty as a carrying case.

2″ x 2″ rigid plastic coin holder with air-tight seal. Comes in about a dozen sizes to fit any coin. Attractive but bulky if you use a lot of them. (Photo courtesy of Whitman Coin Products.)

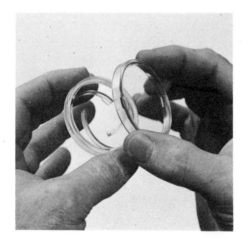

"ReMarkable" rigid clear plastic, variable-size coin holder. Coin is suspended between screw-on cover and holder to prevent abrasion. (Photo courtesy of Remark Industries, Inc.)

Mahogany cabinets with anything from 10 to 20 shallow trays or more, each with round depressions to hold small to large coins, are used extensively in England, where they are made. However, not too many collectors in the United States care for them. Nonetheless, they do offer easy visibility of an entire series of coins all at the same time. All pertinent information concerning the individual coin is written on a round "ticket" which is placed under the coin.

As you browse in the coin shops or see advertisements on the subject, no doubt you will find the method of storing your numismatic material that suits you best. Remember, too, that regardless of how you store it, it should be kept in a safe place that burglars won't find readily!

Cataloguing Your Coins

You will want to maintain a record of the coins in your collection and, whether you do so on 3" x 5" index cards contained in a file box, or on 8½" x 11" sheets slipped into a loose leaf binder, here is the basic information which should be included for each coin:

1. Country of origin.
2. Denomination and date (if any).
3. Mint mark if any.
4. Type of metal or alloy.
5. Grading of coin.
6. Purchased from.
7. Date purchased.
8. Cost.
9. Remarks.

If your coins happen to be foreign, whether old or contemporary, wherever a monarch's portrait is shown or issued during the reign, the first item can be amplified by indicating the monarch's name and regnal years, such as *Great Britain:* Elizabeth II (1952–) or, *Roman Empire:* Augustus (29 B.C.–14 A.D.). In fact many republics portray their current presidents on their coinage, and their names and dates or years of administration should also be recorded.

Ancient and medieval coins, as well as pieces from well into the middle of the nineteenth century including many issued by the United States, often vary considerably. This was the result of using dies cut by hand, about which we will say more later. Thus, you may wish to list the lettering as it appears on your piece. And because even the portraiture varied with the diecutter's skill, you could record that by making rubbings of those coins. Some collectors who are also "shutterbugs" and have the necessary camera equipment photograph parts of their collections for further identification.

In the beginning though, you may find that the basics are all you need to worry about.

Displaying Your Collection

One of the nice things that makes any kind of collecting especially interesting is the opportunity to show others what you collect, even those who know nothing about your subject. Unfortunately, a couple of hundred Lincoln cents of different dates neatly arranged in folders are not going to have too much appeal to your non-collector friends who might well say, "They all look alike." But when you assemble the coins of your country by type, as we have discussed, you will have a collection that *is* interesting to almost everyone. Most people have seen little else than the coins current in their lifetime and will welcome the chance to examine older ones. Everybody likes to look at the unusual.

When you are ready to show your coins at your coin club (because that is partly what these clubs are for), try to liven up the display with a bit of commentary concerning it. There is always a story in coins. If you can find one that suits your exhibit, the other members will be glad to look and to hear even though they may have far more important material than yours—or specialize in something entirely different.

There is nothing more deadly than a mass of coins laid out one next to the other with nothing to relieve the monotony. This writer has seen beautiful material on exhibit which for this reason has failed to capture the viewer's full interest. Also, there is the artistically arranged grouping that still conveys nothing to the beholder mainly because the exhibitor makes no attempt to describe, however tersely, what is being shown.

Next opportunity you have, attend a coin convention and examine the exhibits. Chances are that those which interest you most will be quite informative as well as attractively arranged. If these exhibits are in competition for awards, most likely they will rate high.

As a rule, exhibition judges use a point system—so many points for completeness of the display, condition of the material, information concerning it, arrangement, and the like. At formal exhibitions, numismatic material is generally displayed in shallow, glass-topped cases measuring about 21″ x 33″. These in turn are placed on tables at a level so that the viewer may conveniently look down into them as he walks through the hall. Of course, sometimes the nature of the material requires a wall or panel display.

An exhibit is usually composed of related items and, when properly presented, will be built around a central theme. You may not be an expert on much of what is shown but, if the exhibitor has done a proper job, you will want to linger long enough to study and enjoy what you see.

At meetings of coin clubs, the members' exhibits are considerably less formal. Often, they will be on specified "topics of the evening," and sometimes an award may be given for the one judged to be best. Even here where informality prevails, be sure that what you show is properly identified and neatly arranged.

If you have the true collector's instinct, you will want to see and hear what others are doing in the field even though their specialties may be far afield from your own. Besides, you are going to get ideas from them. That is the advantage of being with "kindred spirits" in the enjoyment of your hobby.

Really Old Coins Still Available to Collectors

Non-collectors often express their surprise that centuries-old coins are still obtainable. In point of fact, many of them are found in beautiful condition. The reason is that from earliest times, before the era of banks and during wars or periods of general unrest, people buried their treasure in the earth for safekeeping. Others may have hidden theirs in the walls or floors of their houses. Sometimes they forgot about the cache or died before they had a chance to retrieve it. Often centuries later, a farmer plowing a field, or a workman demolishing an old structure, might uncover a hidden receptacle and the coins it contained.

Finding these ancient hoards is more common in the parts of the world which had old civilizations, such as Europe, Asia, and North Africa. We do hear occasionally, though, of finds traced to our colonial and Civil War periods. From time to time excavations for new buildings will bring to light early coins. More often than not these were simply lost pieces rather than deliberately hidden treasure. Examination of the cornerstones of old public buildings finally torn down has sometimes brought to light a handful of coins and other mementos placed there at the dedication ceremony.

The sea often gives up lost treasure. Coins from old wrecks are occasionally washed ashore on our own coasts as well as elsewhere in the world. In recent times full-scale salvage operations have been successful where ships are known to have foundered, such as off our Florida coast and in the West Indies.

Because finds of ancient Roman coins and others are constantly being turned up in Europe and the rest of the old world, it is still possible to obtain some of them at modest prices when they appear on the market.

Scholars always wish to document coin hoards. They ascertain the archaeological details such as the depth of the find spot, the type and condition of the container, and details of any other objects found there. The coins themselves usually permit an educated guess as to the date of deposition, which sometimes can be made with remarkable accuracy, give or take a few years. Much history which was previously a matter of conjecture has been documented from coin hoards. Occasionally the "provenance," or origin, of a coin you may buy will be stated on the envelope as being from a particular hoard.

Lastly, coin collecting in modern times has been pursued as a hobby for at least a few hundred years. Accumulations are usually disposed of at auction or by outright sale. Thus, some old and rare coins have "pedigrees" which can be traced, in many instances, to private collections going back perhaps 100 years or more.

The Beginnings of Coinage

The first actual coins used as a medium of exchange were issued in Lydia, a city-state of ancient Greece, about the seventh century B.C. These were simply lumps of electrum, a white gold found naturally alloyed with silver, and impressed with the city's badge or symbol (in this case, the forepart of a lion) on one side, while the other was left blank. In effect, the issuing authority guaranteed the purity and weight of this money so that it would be readily acceptable in trade. Before this, merchants had to weigh and test each raw lump separately, which obviously took a great deal of time. It is no wonder that coined money caught on so readily.

As the years progressed, all the important Greek cities and overseas colonies not only issued their own coins but improved on the basic idea. The most familiar of the early emblems were the Athenian amphora or wine jar and Aegina's turtle, later the tortoise or land turtle. About 550 B.C., the fabled King Croesus of Lydia ordered a pure gold coinage, following it up with silver.

After coins had been "uniface" (one sided) for a long time, the next step was the use of punch marks on the reverse. Later, the Athenians departed from this simple mark by stamping their reverses with the now famous owl, the profile head of their patron goddess Athena being on the obverse. The owl pieces caught on everywhere and circulated freely across much of Europe and Asia.

From very early times, coin designs displayed an as yet unsurpassed artistry. Some of the greatest sculptors of the ancient world were responsible for them. We know many of their names, including Herakleidas and Kimon who lived about 400 B.C. and worked in Greek Syracuse and Catania in Sicily.

COINS OF THE ANCIENT GREEKS

Lydia: gold Stater of Croesus, c. 564 B.C. (Lion and bull on obverse.)

Aegina: silver didrachm, c. 480 B.C. The sea turtle on obverse, badge of the city.

Athens: silver didrachm, c. 490 B.C. Head of Athena on obverse. Reverse shows famous owl of Athens.

Athens: silver tetradrachm, c. 510 B.C. Gorgon on obverse. Lion's head reverse.

Acanthus: silver tetradrachm, c. 530–480 B.C. Attic type.

Pergamum: silver tetradrachm of Attalus I, 269–197 B.C.

Acanthus, Macedon: tetradrachm, 530–480 B.C.

Neapolis (Naples) silver stater with Gorgon's head, 511–500 B.C.

Rhodes, tetradrachm, c. 406 B.C. Helios/Rose

Mausollus, tetradrachm, c. 360 B.C. Apollo; Zeus standing, at reverse.

Larisa, didrachm, 400–344 B.C.

Rhodes, didrachm, c. 408 B.C. Helios with rose on reverse.

Aenus, tetradrachm, c. 400 B.C. Hermes on obverse; goat on reverse.

Mausollus, tetradrachm, c. 360 B.C.

Chalcis, sixth century B.C., tetradrachm. Eagle on obverse. Wheel on reverse.

Macedon: silver tetradrachm of Alexander III (the Great), 336–323 B.C. Zeus sits on throne at reverse.

Coining Techniques — Ancient, Medieval, and Modern

Hand Hammering

The Greeks were the innovators of this original technique for producing coins and also developed a method for preparing the blanks. Their hammering procedure, at least, continued without essential change in Europe and elsewhere until about the end of the eighteenth century A.D.—a period of about 2,500 years, a fantastic record.

The process required little more than a hammer, powered by a good right arm. A handcarved intaglio design on a thick piece of bronze (later iron, and still later, steel) served as the obverse die which was placed in a groove in an anvil. The reverse design was carved in the flat working end of a punch. Cast metal blanks, more or less circular, were beaten to a proper thickness and adjusted to required weight, then later heated in a small furnace to soften them. Next, the blank was lifted with tongs and placed on top of the reverse die, which was held firmly in its groove.

The actual striking required that the punch be held with one hand, with the reverse die in position over the blank and the hammer brought down on it sharply two or three times. The finished coin, with its design impressed on both sides, was later removed from the matrix with tongs.

Most of the coins so produced had highly irregular edges resulting from the hammer blows, which naturally caused the softened metal to spread in all directions. Again, when the blanks were incorrectly positioned between the dies, the completed coins lacked part of their designs and perhaps the peripheral inscriptions. Nor was there any special attempt during the blanking stage to make the pieces really round to start with. They were at best crudely fashioned from flattened lumps or strips of metal. To adjust to standard weight, the old moneyers either filed or pared metal from the edges, or filled in with plugs if underweight, making the coins even more shapeless.

A medieval moneyer's workshop showing the operations of blanking, hand hammering, and trimming. The boy's job was to remove the completed coin from the die and place it in the basket, right foreground. The iron-bound box, center, was for the "Trail of the Pyx"—samples of each lot being placed there for later examination.

Machined or "Milled" Coins

Sometime about the year 1500 A.D. the Italians refined the hand screw press, adapting it for the striking of medals. In fact, Leonardo da Vinci (1452–1519) is known to have improved it, as well as to design a rolling mill and a cutting press for stamping out blanks. Benvenuto Cellini (1500–1571) also used such machinery for some of the coins he produced at ducal and papal courts. However adequate this was for medals, the earliest machinery was still cumbersome and slow and thus not satisfactory for regular coinage where high volume production was required.

Early "milled" coining operations; a hand screw press, c. 1700. A powerful tug on the heavy lever swung it around, thus turning the screw and exerting great pressure on the coin blank situated between the dies. Safety engineering was not thought of at the time and mint workers were usually short a finger or two.

FIRST COINING PRESS AT THE U.S. MINT, 1792

A screw press powered solely by the strong arms of the coiners, first used in 1792 before the mint buildings were completed, to produce trial coins. It also produced many of the cents and half cents in 1793. Larger presses were built by 1795, so this one was probably retired after striking fewer than 300,000 coins. Hand power was the sole means of propulsion throughout the 40-year life of the first mint. Only a million coins were produced in the first eight years of operation. (Photo courtesy of the Bureau of the Mint by Larry Stevens, Coinpics.)

Many experimental runs of milled coins were produced in England, France, Italy, and elsewhere over the next hundred years or so, but hand hammering remained the surest, fastest, and lowest-cost method that could be employed for a long time.

By the end of the seventeenth century, the machine designers overcame the earlier difficulties, developing much faster and more accurate equipment, including a rolling mill driven by a horse plodding around a treadmill. The other new machinery, however, continued to be operated by the strong arms of the mint workers. Operating characteristics were thus sufficient to bring the milled coining method to reasonable levels of efficiency. Incidentally, the word "mill" referred to the machinery itself and had nothing to do with the reed marks on

Rolling and coiling operations at the U.S. Mint, Philadelphia. The coiled strip will later be processed into coins. (Photo courtesy of the Bureau of the Mint by Lawrence S. Williams, Inc.)

the edges of coins such as those on U.S. quarters, which are sometimes erroneously called "milling."

An important feature of the new machinery was a collar which surrounded the blank when seated in the press. This kept the struck coin from spreading to an irregular shape. It remained fully round, or nearly so. At the same time, this collar permitted impress of edge markings, whether reeded, as mentioned above, or lettered.

Over a long period coining machinery gradually improved and the manpower and horsepower needed to drive it gave way to waterpower, steam, and finally electricity. Today's high-speed coining equipment at the newly constructed U.S. Mint in Philadelphia is technologically perfect (if anything can be) and is completely automated to produce the perfectly round, well-struck, and stackable coins you have in your pocket. The background for its perfection, however, goes straight to the machine designers of the seventeenth century.

It may be of interest to mention here that even though machinery replaced the old hand-hammering method in Europe before 1700, its use continued in some independent states of India into the middle of the nineteenth century, and in some Arab sheikdoms as late as the first decade or two of the twentieth. It is still possible to find some of the coins thus produced, which can be interesting conversation pieces.

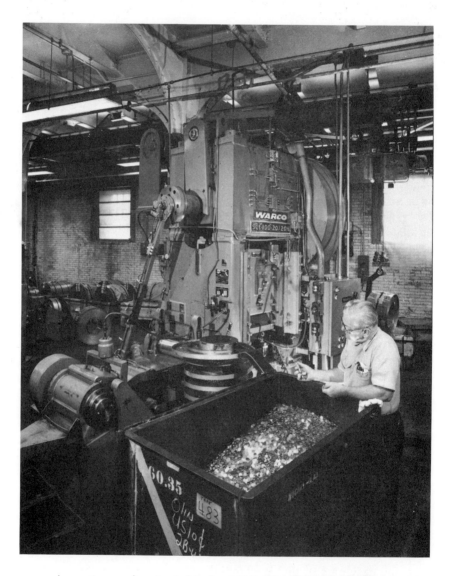

Inspecting newly cut coin blanks at U.S. Mint, Philadelphia. (Photo courtesy of the Bureau of the Mint by Lawrence S. Williams, Inc.)

Gilroy Roberts, right, ninth engraver of the United States Mint, worked on the model of the John F. Kennedy half dollar, adapted from a presidential medal designed by Roberts in 1961.

Frank Gasparro, assistant to the chief engraver, designed the reverse of the Kennedy half dollar.

Coins of the Romans and the Byzantines

By the middle of the third century B.C. the Romans became the inheritors of the Greek monetary tradition. Sometime earlier, however, they had used a cumbersome cast coinage known as the "Aes Grave," which by weight was originally about one pound avoirdupois. This together with its fractions (the semis, triens, and quadrans) seemed to suffice as a trade medium while Rome was simply a small and locally oriented city-state of central Italy.

The first struck pieces issued by Rome in silver, gold, and bronze were modeled after those of the Italo-Greek coinages of southern Italy and Sicily. About 187 B.C., however, the famous "denarius," or silver penny, appeared. It was of thinner fabric than the Greek coins and bore typically Roman motifs. For the remainder of the Republican era, the bronze coinage was gradually reduced in size, nor was it of great importance by that time. The *aureus,* or gold penny, was issued about 90 B.C. for the first time, although Rome had had other gold coins for a hundred years earlier on a sporadic basis.

Usually the coins of the Roman Republic had the heads of various gods and goddesses, including that of Roma, personified as obverse designs. Later pieces bore the portrait heads of consuls and others of the period.

Under the empire which began with Augustus in 29 B.C., the obverses as a rule contained the portrait of the reigning emperor while the reverses showed deities or personifications. In fact, the reverse designs were often used as a means of propaganda to ingratiate the emperor with the people, calling attention to his professed virtues and promoting his programs.

Of particular delight to collectors of the Roman series are the large, thick bronze sesterces struck during the empire, most of them with handsome portraits of the reigning emperor. The silver denarius continued during the Empire, although in its final years it lost much of

Silver denarius 89–88 B.C., C.Vibius Pansa (moneyer). Head of Apollo; reverse: Goddess Minerva in quadriga.

Silver denarius c. 57 B.C. L.Roscius Fabatus (moneyer). Head of Juno. Girl feeding serpent on reverse.

Silver denarius 90–89 B.C., L.Piso L.F. Frugi (moneyer). Head of Apollo; reverse: naked horseman.

Aes Grave—Cast bronze coinage c. 220–205 B.C. This is shown in reduced size.

Three denarii of Julius Caesar, dictator of Rome 48–44 B.C.

Early denarii of Augustus Caesar as Emperor, 31 B.C.–14 A.D.

its precious metal content and finally gave place to a bronze coinage, at first coated with a slight film of silver, called the *antoninianus.*

Roman mints were established even in remote parts of the empire. When the Western Empire collapsed in 476 A.D., the Eastern or Byzantine Empire based at Constantinople continued the coinage. The Roman characteristics of realistic portraiture and design, however, quickly gave place to stylized, angular effects. Indeed, there were many instances of the inscriptions being given in both Greek and Latin letters, even in the same word, during the transition period.

The Byzantine coinage, with a charm and beauty all its own, lasted until 1453 A.D., when Constantinople fell to the Turks. Its pieces greatly influenced the new national states of Europe when they settled down after the Dark Ages to develop their own new civilization out of the chaos left in the wake of the ruin of the Western Empire.

The Byzantine series in gold, silver, and bronze is a very broad one that ranged over a period of a thousand years. It should be of greater interest to collectors than it is at present. Many of these coins can be procured at modest cost. In fact even the gold *solidi* and *besants* are not expensive in relation to gold pieces of other series.

BRONZE COINS

OF THE

ROMAN EMPIRE

Sestertius of Marcus Aurelius, 161–180 A.D.

Sestertius of Titus, 79–91 A.D.   Sestertius of Trajan, 98–117 A.D.

Sestertius of Antoninus Pius, 138–161 A.D.   As of Trajan, 98–117 A.D.

BYZANTINE EMPIRE

Solidi and other gold denominations, sixth to ninth centuries A.D.

Medieval and Renaissance Coins

The Medieval Period

Art in coinage as the Greeks and Romans understood the term disappeared at the breakup of the Western Roman Empire. Coins of the so-called Dark Ages in Europe were crudely designed and executed. Many of the inscriptions, badly blundered, are difficult or impossible to read. This situation continued until the eighth century, even though the Byzantines in the East had independently been striking attractive pieces according to their new art form and which the new Moslem states had adapted to their purpose.

As Europe entered the medieval period in history, the coinage became revitalized. Pepin [Pippin the Short (752–768)] of the Frankish kingdom introduced a new silver coinage of thin fabric weighing about 18 grains (approx. 1¼ grams) and roughly ¾″ in diameter. Called the *denar,* it was of neat design and workmanship. It was quickly adapted by the Anglo-Saxon kingdoms across the channel, who brought this coin to its highest flowering as the silver penny of England.

Thus, the Roman denarius, variously called on the Continent the *denar, denier, dinar, pfennig,* etc., has survived in name if not in substance. To this day, the symbol for a penny in England has been a "d."

This silver penny and others more or less like it, almost wafer-thin, were the largest coins of Europe until close to the end of the thirteenth century. In the agrarian economy that prevailed in the Middle Ages, there was little need for anything larger. These were the times when a prize sheep was worth 12 pence and an acre of the best land in England might have been sold for four pennies more.

Merchants and kings did require larger denominations for their transactions. In England, for example, they did their figuring in pounds sterling and shillings as well as pence. But these denominations were not to be coined for hundreds of years. They were known as "money of account." (If this seems unusual to you, remember that we in the

52

United States also have a money of account, although most people don't realize it. Ours is the *mil* worth ¹/₁₀th of a cent.)

For a long time during this period the coin reverses bore not only the name of the town of minting but the *moneyer's* name as well. This placed the responsibility for correct weight and fineness directly on those authorized to coin at the various mints. There were very severe penalties—mutilation or death—inflicted when a moneyer played hanky-panky with the king's coin.

"Clipping" was also a grave problem. Since the coin edges on all of this hammered money were uneven, many pared small slivers from them. When they obtained enough silver in this manner it was melted down and disposed of on the medieval black market. The coins themselves went back into circulation and eventually the last holder lost out because their value had been lessened—sometimes by as much as 20 percent. When clippers were caught, they too suffered the penalties mentioned above. The practice did not die out, however, until coins became really round and carried edge markings.

The larger coin finally struck by the states of thirteenth century Europe was worth four silver pennies. This *grosso,* first struck in Milan, was the *gros* of France, the *groat* of England, and the *groschen* of Germany. But as the European economy progressed, still larger silver coins and also gold pieces put in their appearance. Gold florins, sequins (zecchini), and ducats were issued in northern Italy in the middle of the thirteenth century and circulated throughout Europe in international trade. These competed with the similar gold besants and solidi of the Byzantine emperors which for a long time were the only coins available in the yellow metal. By the fourteenth century, gold coin was commonplace in most of the European states, although the rank and file found the small silver pieces ample for their needs.

COINS OF THE

MEDIEVAL PERIOD

(Silver Unless Stated)

Axum (Ethiopia) fourth century A.D.

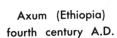

Mercia (Anglo–Saxon England); penny of King Offa (757–796).

Denier of Charlemagne (768–814).

Denier of Pippin of Aquitaine (839–852).

Wessex (Anglo–Saxon England); penny of Alfred the Great (871–899).

Denier of Pippin the Great, 752–768 (Father of Charlemagne).

Bohemia; denar of Bratislaw I (1037–1055).

Bracteate of Thuringia, Germany, early thirteenth century. Bracteates were usually of silver and so wafer-thin that the impression of the obverse design showed through to the reverse thus repeating the obverse, incuse. They had the approximate value of the denars of the period.

Groat (fourpence); Edward III of England, 1327–1377. This type, first issued in 1289, changed little over a period of 200 years.

France: Petit blanc of Charles VII, 1422–1461.

Florence (Itay): Fiorino d'argent (silver florin) fifteenth century.

Florence (Italy): Fiorino d'oro (gold florin) fifteenth century.

Coins of the Renaissance

By the end of the fifteenth century, most coins took on a new appearance. The Italian Renaissance influenced the discontinuance of the archaic, stylized coin designs which had dominated the medieval period. In their place came handsome, recognizable portraiture. If you cared to start a collection of coins with realistic portraits of the monarchs of the European nations, you would be able to start no earlier than with those reigning about the years somewhat before and after 1500. These would include Henry VII of England, Francis I of France, and Ferdinand and Isabella of Spain.

Starting at about this time, we find many larger silver pieces. In fact, this was the period that set the stage for modern coinage.

COINS OF THE RENAISSANCE PERIOD

Milan, silver Testone of Duke Galeazzo Maria Sforza (1466–1476) and right, one of Ludovico Sforza, 1494–1499.

England, Henry VII (1485–1509); silver profile groat.

England, Henry VIII (1509–1547); silver Testoon. Later this denomination was called the shilling.

England, Henry VIII; gold Sovereign of 20 shillings.

Dollar–Sized Silver Coins

Dollar-sized silver coins were first produced in 1484 in the Tyrol by Archduke Sigismund and were equivalent in value to the gold gulden of the time. While other rulers issued such pieces from that time on, it was the Joachimstaler struck in 1520 by the Counts of Schlick in the Joachimstal in Bohemia which really set the stage for these large coins.

Their name came from *tal,* German for valley, and the name of St. Joachim, the patron saint of the area. His portrait was on the obverse, with a lion backing him up on the reverse. The coin's name was shortened to *Taler* and was the derivation of our dollar, the Italian tallero, the daalder of the Netherlands, and others.

The kingdoms, principalities and duchies of Europe, not to forget the free cities, counties, electorates of the Holy Roman Empire, bishoprics and archbishoprics, all had had their own coinage for many centuries. But the larger denomination seemed to give them further incentive to make the mints work overtime striking a profusion of talers. Besides regular currency pieces, there were birth talers, death talers, marriage talers, hunting, and mining talers. Some, called "broad" talers, were of wider diameter than usual but much thinner. There were also multiples —double and triple talers.

Most of the German talers, of the earlier period particularly, were very ornate and beautifully executed, issued as they were when baroque art flourished.

Maria Theresa of Austria struck a taler in 1780 which for some reason captured the fancy of people even in far distant lands—so much so that it continued to be coined for over 150 years without change of design, even of date. It circulated in some of the Arab countries until quite recently, and still may in isolated sections, as the people preferred it to any other currency.

In France the *Ecu blanc* (white shield or crown) and in England the silver crown, struck for the first time in 1551, contested the talers of the Continent. And the Spanish milled dollar, which gave its name to our own coin because it was so popular during and after the colonial period, circulated freely. But for sheer beauty and general numismatic interest, the talers of Germany have always been favorites of collectors.

Joachimstaler, 1526; Counts of Schlick.

England, silver Crown, Edward VI dated 1551. (The first dollar-size coin of England.)

Brunswick-Wolfenbuettel; Duke Henry Julius, thick double taler dated 1607.

Brunswick-Wolfenbuettel; Duke Christian, thick hybrid double taler, dated 1620 and 1626.

Bohemia, Friedrich of Pfalz, taler 1621.

Tuscany, Grand Duke Cosimo III; tollero 1718.

Savoy, King Victor Amadeo III; scudo of 1773.

Mexico, Ferdinand II, 1820; 8 reales.

Die Engraving, Errors, and Resulting Varieties

For most of the history of coining, coins have been struck from dies, although the Romans and the Chinese at certain periods in their history had a cast coinage, produced by pouring molten metal into molds.

Until comparatively recent times, dies were engraved by hand and in actual size. A wide variety of punches and graving tools were used to rout out or cut away the "dead" metal as needed in order to form the design and inscription.

Since duplicate dies were always required, often in considerable quantity, they had to be copied freehand—where possible, from the original master dies. However, there were always variations. Some die engravers (also called die sinkers) were much more skilled than others. Then again, certain of them had a way of garnishing the other fellow's design with "improvements" of their own. Also, as dies became worn, some were recut to continue their useful life a little longer.

There were also errors in spelling. "LIHERTY" for "LIBERTY" on the U.S. large cent of 1796 is a typical example of this. It appears on a single die and evidently the engraver did not notice he had pulled the wrong punch. For crude workmanship, we have the "Silly" head and "Booby" head varieties of the 1839 cent. You have only to see them in photograph to realize why they were so named by numismatists.

Our early coinage is replete with such varieties resulting from hand-cut replacement dies. However, since the latter part of the nineteenth century, machinery has taken over the work of engraving both the master and duplicate dies. Nowadays a large clay model is prepared by the sculptor, cast in plaster and electrotyped. This is then reduced mechanically by a machine which reproduces the design at the end of a steel bar or hub. Duplicate dies are made from the master in quantities as large as desired, the last being, for all practical purposes, the same as the first.

Modern technology has thus reduced the chances of turning up new varieties within coin types—to the utter annoyance, of course, of those who like to collect them. But they do occur, however infrequently. (See the "double die" cent of 1955.)

Other than early die sinkers' errors or interpretations, you will find we have had occasional authorized changes in design, sometimes within the same year. Also, dies of one year have been used in the next after a recutting, such as the dime of 1942 over '41. There are Lincoln cents of 1960 which were discovered to have dates in two sizes—large and small. In the early years, die breaks were not infrequent and resulted in striking flaws in the coins produced from them. With the electronic sensing devices available now, however, a broken die means instantaneous stoppage of the press. Thus, spoiled coins can be watched for and discarded—unless someone takes them from the mint illegally.

As we have indicated, mint errors in the coinage produced by modern machinery are sought after by many collectors and usually command a substantial premium because they are the exception. However, the converse is true in the case of the old hand-hammered coins. These are found quite frequently either off-center or double-struck (inherent characteristics of the process) and accordingly their desirability to the collector is lessened. Properly centered, clearly impressed pieces are preferred. The reason is easy to understand: Perfectly minted hand-hammered coins are hard to come by and therefore prized; naturally they cost much more.

DIE ERRORS
AND VARIETIES

Close-up view of the small cent of 1955 showing the "double-die" error at the Philadelphia Mint. It commands a very high price.

Double-struck Buffalo nickel.

The Buffalo on the nickel of 1937 (Denver Mint) turned up with only three legs and is now a recognized variety. Trouble is that others have confounded the issue by removing a leg from the usual type, to defraud collectors. So watch out.

Note the variations in these three U.S. Large Cents of 1839 resulting from their having been struck from different dies, each cut by hand. Many collectors specialize in die varieties and errors.

Early Coins of Colonial America

Our mother country did not supply enough coins to the colonists of North America for normal currency needs. What coins appeared on these shores quickly returned to Europe in payment for supplies purchased there. Of course beaver skins, tobacco, and other commodities had been used on a barter basis when trading with the Indians, who also valued wampum or shell money highly. These items also passed as currency among the colonists themselves for a long time because there was nothing else.

To ease this situation, the General Court of New England issued the "NE" shilling and fractional pieces in 1652. This first hard money of Colonial America was blank except for the letters NE on the obverse and XII (for 12 pence, which equalled a shilling) on the reverse or VI or III in the smaller denominations. Their extreme simplicity of design made them easy prey to counterfeiters and they were replaced by the more elaborate Willow Tree, Oak Tree, and Pine Tree pieces.

The new coins, all dated 1652 even though issued through 1682, were illegal as far as the English authorities were concerned. In fact, the new king, Charles II, who ascended the throne in 1660, opposed them vehemently. The 1652 date was a clever way of removing responsibility, for who could tell from it when the coins were really struck?

At the end of the seventeenth century and continuing during the eighteenth before the American Revolution, various coins (properly called tokens) were circulated in most of the colonies to help alleviate the continuing severe shortage of regular currency. Produced generally in England and Ireland, mostly in copper and occasionally in silver, they were valued from a farthing (a quarter of an English penny) up to a shilling. Some were produced under patent from the king of England, but probably most were not.

With the advent of the American Revolution and until the new Federal Constitution became effective, many of the new states issued their own coinages, principally of copper cents. There were also token coins issued by merchants and, of course, a whole series of Washington token pieces was inevitable. These all bore likenesses of the father of our country, some unrecognizable, and were struck during the years 1783 to 1795.

EARLY COINS
OF COLONIAL AMERICA

John Higley (or Granby, Conn.) copper tokens dated 1737.

Pine Tree Shilling dated 1652.

N.E. Shilling (12 pence) dated 1652.

Rosa Americana token, twopence about 1722. Supplied under patent from King George I by William Wood.

Maryland (Lord Baltimore
Shilling) dated 1658.

Nova Eborac (New York)
copper token dated 1787.

Connecticut token dated 1788.

Washington piece (Liverpool
Halfpenny) 1791.

New Jersey copper cent dated 1786.

Brasher Doubloon, 1787: A gold piece of about 408 grains, equivalent roughly to the Spanish doubloon worth approximately $16, and produced by Ephraim Brasher, a New York jeweler. It is excessively rare.

Mints of the United States

The word "mint" derives from the old English *mynet*, meaning money. In turn this comes from the Latin *moneta*, which in ancient Rome was the surname of the goddess Juno Moneta, wife of Jupiter. It was in her temple in Rome that silver coins were struck as early as 269 B.C. Although the Greeks invented the coining process much earlier, posterity did not grant them the honor of taking *their* word for it.

The main United States Mint is in Philadelphia, as it has been since the inception of official coinage in this country. Besides the Philadelphia facility, six others have operated at various times as shown below. Only the Denver and San Francisco branch mints continue today, although the latter, which was closed for general purposes in 1955, later reopened (1968) to strike cents, special coins such as proofs, and uncirculated pieces, including the Eisenhower dollars.

• Location of Mint	• Dates	• Mint Mark
• Philadelphia	• 1792 to date	• None except on nickels of the years 1942 to 1945 when the letter P was used to indicate wartime change of alloy.
• New Orleans	• 1838–1861, then 1870–1893	• O
• Charlotte, N.C.	• 1838–1861	• C (on gold coins only)
• Dahlonega, Ga.	• 1838–1861	• D (on gold coins only)
• San Francisco	• 1854–1955 1968 to date	• S
• Carson City, Nev.	• 1870–1893	• CC
• Denver	• 1906 to date	• D

Most coins, year by year, have been struck at more than one mint, and the mint of issue can be distinguished on the coin by its letter-designation (or lack of it, as in the case of Philadelphia). The mark is usually found on the reverse, but not always; the Lincoln cents, for example, have carried it on the obverse under the date since their inception. Commencing in 1968, however, mint marks for all other U.S. coin denominations were relocated to the obverse, thus making it easier to spot them.

The Charlotte and Dahlonega mints were originally opened so that gold from the mines discovered in those areas could be brought there for coining but the veins were finally worked out and these branch mints became unnecessary. The fact that "D" stands for both Dahlonega and Denver causes no confusion in reading a coin since the former mint produced only gold coins—and those long before Denver was placed in operation.

The old branch mints fulfilled their purpose and were closed when coining presses became faster and transport improved. Nowadays, for ordinary purposes, the Philadelphia and Denver mints can supply all the coins the country's economy requires.

The place of minting of a coin is extremely important to the collector. The reason is that the branch mints usually strike much smaller quantities than Philadelphia, and therefore their coins will have greater rarity.

Many collectors are never satisfied unless they can obtain a piece of a given denomination and year from each of the mints where they were struck, whether old or new coins. Since it is not the purpose of this book to supply complete tabulations of coins struck year by year at the various mints, you can find them if you wish in the "Red Book" mentioned earlier and in a number of other publications.

As an example, however, a full set of Lincoln cents from the year 1909 would have to contain four pieces. These would include 1909 (no mark and thus from Philadelphia), 1909S (San Francisco), *and* two others, one from each of these mints with the initials of the designer, V.D.B., on the reverse. (Victor D. Brenner's initials were removed after appearing on a limited quantity.) Of the 1909S-VDB cent, the records show that only 484,000 were struck. On the other hand, the 1909 Philadelphia VDB cent had a production of about 28 million pieces. Of those without the initials, the Philadelphia output was 73 million and that of San Francisco less than 2 million. The 1909S-VDB cent is a very expensive coin to buy in any condition.

Coin Types of the United States

FUGIO CENT

The U.S. Mint in Philadelphia was created on April 2, 1792, even though the Federal Constitution became effective in 1789. However, the Board of Treasury, acting under the powers vested in it by the Continental Congress had, on April 21, 1787, authorized the production of 300 tons of copper coins.

The result was the "Fugio" cents, all dated 1787 and so-called because the word "Fugio" (I fly) appears on the obverse. This and the reverse legend, "Mind Your Business," are generally attributed to Benjamin Franklin. The coin, also known as the Franklin cent, was produced by a contractor in New Haven, Connecticut, from dies cut by Abel Buel of that city.

The chain of 13 links on the reverse, the obverse design of a sun dial and sun's rays, as well as the legends "We are One" and "Mind Your Business," were obviously adapted from the Continental Dollar of 1776, specimens of which, struck in several metals, are now considered patterns since few were ever circulated.

Many varieties of the Fugio cents are known. A few pairs of dies are still extant, having been found in 1858. At that time, they were used for "restrikes" which are now themselves rare. However, it is still possible to find original Fugios in good condition at reasonable cost. A collector of U.S. coins should certainly try to acquire a specimen of this first official issue, even though it was not struck at a government mint.

Large Cents

The earliest of the government-minted cents were first issued in 1793. They were considerably greater in diameter and thickness than those of the present day, as the same size illustrations will show, and were struck from almost pure copper. These "large cents," as they were called, continued in slightly reduced size until 1857 and were minted in seven basic types.

U.S. LARGE CENTS

Liberty head with flowing hair; chain-type reverse, 1793.

Liberty Cap type; wreath reverse, 1793-1796.

Draped Bust type, 1796-1807.

Turban (or Classic Head type), 1808-1814.

Coronet type, 1816-1839.

Braided Hair type, 1840-1857.

Small Cents

Minting of small cents was authorized on February 21, 1857, and the first type was issued through 1858. These were called the Flying Eagle or "white" cents because of the silvery color resulting from an alloy of 88 percent copper and 12 percent nickel. A small quantity of the type dated 1856 was actually struck and all these are quite rare. The Flying Eagles were replaced by the head of an Indian girl in 1859. In 1864, the alloy was changed to bronze and the weight reduced from 72 grains to 48, resulting in the coin "fabric" as we have it today.

The Lincoln cents, which superseded the Indians, were struck to commemorate the centennial of his birth in 1909. This familiar type has been with us up to the present with only minute modifications in portrait and lettering, the last in 1969 when the former became slightly smaller. But the reverse was changed completely in 1959 to coincide with the great president's 150th birthday. So in effect it gave us another cent type. Double-die errors in 1955 and 1972 have produced rarities which command large premiums.

U.S. SMALL CENTS

Flying Eagle type, 1856–1858.

Indian Head type, 1859–1909.

Lincoln Head type with Wheat Ears reverse, 1909–1958.

Lincoln Head type with Memorial reverse, 1959 to date.

Nickels

Once you've managed to get your U.S. type collection of cents under control, you will want to branch out to other denominations. How about the nickel for a starter?

The five cent piece or "nickel" was coined for the first time in 1866 from an alloy of 75 percent copper and 25 percent nickel. It bore a shield design which was superseded in 1883 by the Liberty Heads. Incidentally, the initial dies were prepared without the word "Cents," with the result that many of these coins were gilded and passed off to the unsuspecting as five dollar gold pieces. "Cents" was added later, in the first year of issue.

The Indian Head or Buffalo type was issued from 1913 to 1938. Since then the mints have produced the current Jefferson type. Thus, only four coins (not counting the varieties, of course) would give you examples of every nickel the U.S. has issued.

Shield type (rays on reverse), 1866–1867.

Shield type (no rays on reverse), 1867–1883.

Liberty Head type without "cents" on reverse, 1883.

U.S. NICKEL FIVE CENT PIECES

Liberty Head type with "cents" on reverse, 1883–1913.

Indian Head or Buffalo type, 1913–1938.

Jefferson type, 1938 to date.

Dimes

Beginning in 1796, when the first dime (originally called the "disme") was coined, we have had seven basic types, including those from 1798 through 1807 which had more or less the same obverse as the prior ones. Only the reverse shows a radical change—from a realistic to a heraldic eagle.

The earlier dimes were of larger diameter than our present pieces and their silver fineness and overall weight varied at times until 1874, when they were stabilized. 1964 was the last year of a real silver coinage in the U.S. The following year inaugurated the clad coinage.

There are many varieties among the dimes of the early years. In 1853, and again in 1873 and 1874, arrows were placed at the date to indicate change in weight. These were later removed.

U.S. DIMES

Draped Bust type; small realistic eagle reverse, 1796–1797.

Draped Bust type; heraldic eagle reverse, 1798–1807.

Capped Bust type; note motto on ribbon at reverse—*E Pluribus Unum*—1809–1837.

Liberty Seated type, 1837–1891. (Until 1860, stars appeared on the obverse; the ethnic United States of America at reverse.)

Barber or Liberty Head type, 1892–1916.

Winged Liberty Head or Mercury type, 1916–1945.

Roosevelt type, 1946 to date.

Quarters

In the first year of issue, 1796, these coins showed no mark of value. "25C" was later added on the reverse, continuing until 1838 when "QUAR DOL." appeared. This was not spelled out in full until 1892. As with the dimes, the quarters were larger in the early years, being reduced in size in 1831.

The Liberty Seated type may be further broken down into those with arrows at date and rays above the eagle on the reverse. These denote changes in weight. Also, in 1886 the motto "In God We Trust" was added to the reverse on a streamer above the eagle's head.

The design of the Standing Liberty quarter was modified in 1917 and, in 1925 a further change was made. The date was recessed because it had worn off too easily on the earlier pieces of this type.

The Washington quarter marked the 200th anniversary of the first president's birth and was originally planned as a commemorative coin.

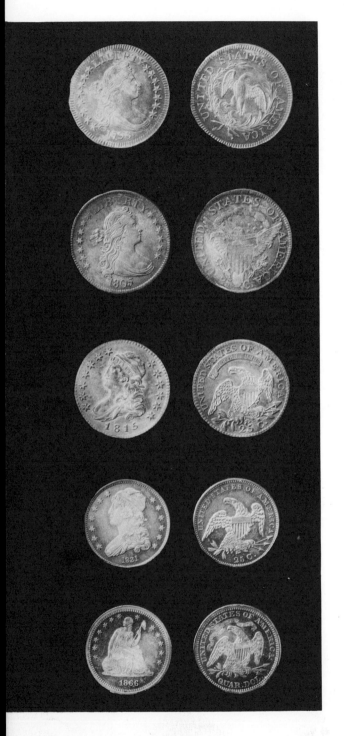

U.S. QUARTER DOLLARS

Draped Bust type, small, realistic eagle reverse, 1796.

Draped Bust type; heraldic eagle reverse, 1804–1807.

Capped Bust type, large size, 1815–1828.

Capped Bust type, reduced size; no motto on reverse, 1831–1838

Liberty Seated type, 1838–1891. The illustration shows the earliest date (1866) which included the legend "In God We Trust" on the ribbon at reverse.

Barber or Liberty Head type, 1892–1916.

Standing Liberty type, 1916–1930.   Washington type, 1932 to date.

Half Dollars

Many of the old half dollars are still obtainable at prices within reach of the average collector, in some instances even in superior condition.

Until 1836, the edges were marked "FIFTY CENTS OR HALF A DOLLAR," but all succeeding coins were given reed marks on the edges, as we have them now. There were many varieties within the same year of issue on the older pieces. The Liberty Seated series followed the pattern of arrows and rays described earlier. The Franklin/Liberty Bell series broke the pattern of carrying a large eagle on the reverse, for the first and only time. However, it featured a small eagle to the right of the bell.

U.S. HALF DOLLARS

Truncated Bust type; small, realistic eagle reverse, 1794–1795.

Draped Bust type with realistic eagle reverse, 1796–1797.

Draped Bust type with heraldic eagle reverse, 1801–1807.

Capped or Turban Head type, 1807–1839.

Variety of above dated 1839 with reeded edge and the mark of value HALF DOL. as shown on reverse.

Liberty Seated type, 1839–1891. Note arrows at date on this piece, indicating change in weight.

Barber of Liberty Head type, 1892–1915.

Liberty Walking type, 1916–1947.

Franklin/Liberty Bell type, 1948–1963.

Kennedy type, 1964 to date.

Silver Dollars

The silver dollar was coined in a handful of types from its inception in 1794, although not consistently, until 1935. It was then discontinued until the advent of the Eisenhower dollar in 1971. As discussed earlier, the silver dollar in modern times has not been regarded as useful currency because of its weight, although many persons have carried one as a pocket-piece.

The 1804 dollar is the rarest U.S. coin. Two types exist and both are thought to have been struck at a later date from old dies. The silver dollar was pegged by law in 1837 at a weight of 412½ grains, fineness .900. This continued until 1965 when all silver was removed from our regular coinage. Thus the "currency" issue of the Eisenhower dollar contains no silver at all.

SILVER DOLLARS (U.S.)

Truncated Bust type; small, realistic eagle at reverse, 1794–1795.

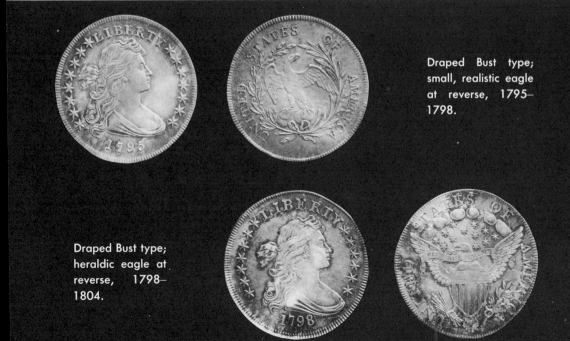

Draped Bust type; small, realistic eagle at reverse, 1795–1798.

Draped Bust type; heraldic eagle at reverse, 1798–1804.

Liberty Seated type without motto, 1840–1866.

Liberty Seated type with motto, 1866–1873.

Liberty Head or Morgan type, 1878–1921.

Eisenhower dollar, 1971 to date.

Peace type, 1921–1935.

TRADE DOLLARS, 1873–1885

Trade Dollars

These coins, weighing 420 grains of .900 fine silver as opposed to our regular silver dollars of 412½ grains, same fineness, were issued from 1873 to 1885 (the last few years as proofs) to compete in the Far East with the then highly-thought-of Mexican peso. They were originally acceptable as legal tender in the U.S. itself but this provision was later withdrawn. In fact, the Trade Dollar is now the only coin of the United States which is not redeemable. Of course, since all of them have substantial numismatic value far beyond their original valuation, it no longer matters.

Long Discontinued Denominations

Bear in mind that, besides the familiar denominations in everyday coinage which you have seen illustrated on the preceding pages, the United States has in the past coined a number of odd denominations, some of which had a comparatively long history while others were extremely short lived.

Our half cents, for example, lasted from 1793 through 1857, while the silver half dimes ranged from 1794 to as late as 1873. We even had a Twenty Cent piece during the years 1875 to 1878. From the length of time it was minted, you can see how popular it was!

Below you see these and the other odd denominations struck in copper (or bronze), nickel, and silver, all of which helped to make change long ago, but no longer.

Half Cents

These copper coins originally weighed 104 grains, but were dropped to 84 grains in 1795. They had the smallest face value of any U.S. coin, but physically they were larger than the present cent. 1796 is the rarest date. There are many varieties. Restrikes were frequent.

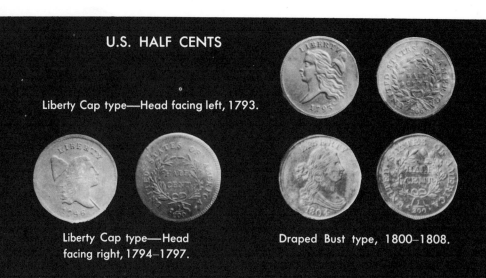

U.S. HALF CENTS

Liberty Cap type—Head facing left, 1793.

Liberty Cap type—Head facing right, 1794–1797.

Draped Bust type, 1800–1808.

Turban or Classic Head type, 1809–
1836.

Braided Hair type, 1840–
1857.

Two Cent Pieces

This piece in bronze was issued for only ten years—from 1864 to
1873—but its claim to fame is the fact that it carried the motto "In God
We Trust" for the first time on a U.S. coin. There was only one type
bearing a shield device on the obverse, quite similar to that on the five
cent shield nickel you have already seen. Two varieties appeared the
first year, the motto having been designed both large and small. In the
last year of issue, only proofs were struck.

**U.S. TWO
CENT PIECES**

Shield type, 1864–
1873.

Three Cent Pieces (Nickel)

The composition of this coin, which was the same as that of the five
cent nickel piece, was 75 percent copper and 25 percent nickel. Weight
was 30 grains. Issued between 1865 and 1889, there was but a single
type of this denomination.

**U.S. THREE CENT
PIECES (Nickel)**

Liberty Head, 1865–
1889.

Three Cent Pieces (Silver)

This was the tiniest official U.S. silver coin and it lasted from 1851 through 1873 in three varieties, although the variations among them are minute. There was thus a period when the American public had a choice of metals when it got three cents in change—or gave it. Weight 11.52 grains, .900 fine.

U.S. THREE CENT PIECES (Silver)

Variety 1 (mint-mark o), 1851–1853.

Variety 2 (three outlines to star), 1854–1858.

Variety 3 (two outlines to star), 1859–1873.

Half Dimes

The half dime was one of the first of our silver coins, having been issued commencing in 1794—or at least they were so dated. They were very similar to the dimes of their series and ranged through the Liberty Seated type, which ended the denomination in 1872. By that time, the five cent nickel, an easier coin to handle, had taken over. Until 1829 the half dime showed no mark of value.

Again, as on the larger silver coins, arrows were placed at the date of the half dimes in 1853 through 1855 to note reduction of weight to 19.2 grains (.900 fine). There were many varieties, particularly in the early coinage.

U.S. HALF DIMES

Half *Disme* of 1792. This and the *Disme*, obsolete term for "Dime" (pronounced *Deem*) were actually patterns for the proposed coinage. Engraved by Robert Birch, they were struck before the regular mint issues.

Liberty with flowing hair, truncated bust; realistic eagle reverse, 1794–1795.

Draped bust of Liberty; reverse similar to above, 1796–1797.

Draped bust; heraldic eagle reverse, 1800–1805.

Capped bust type; motto on ribbon, 1829–1837.

Liberty Seated type, 1837–1872.

Twenty Cent Pieces (Silver)

There was no real reason for issuing this denomination, which had a four year life from 1875 to 1878. Only one type appeared and the public complained so bitterly that it looked and felt so much like the then current quarters (Liberty Seated type) that it was quickly discontinued. There was only a small difference in the diameters of the two coins and the thickness was about the same. Thus, it is easy to see how they were taken in change for the larger denomination. The twenty cent pieces had plain edges as opposed to the reeded edges of the quarters.

If one of your ancestors had had the foresight to keep a few examples of this coin in uncirculated condition, they would be quite valuable now. In any event, specimens of the odd denominations you have seen along with some of the earlier dimes, quarters, and halves, for example, which are not overly expensive in some grades and dates, would help you to form a collection of significance.

U.S. TWENTY CENT PIECES

Liberty Seated type, 1875–1878.

U.S. Gold Coins

The first gold coins struck under authorization of the United States were the Half Eagle or five dollar piece in 1795 and the Eagle (ten dollars) which followed in the same year. The Quarter Eagle ($2.50) was struck for the first time in 1796. In 1849 came the gold dollar and, interestingly, the Double Eagle of $20 as well. So 1849 saw the issuance of the largest and smallest of the regular gold pieces. There was also a three dollar gold piece between 1854 and 1889.

No U.S. gold coins have been struck or circulated since 1933, but it is legal for coin collectors to have them. The first gold coins had a fineness of .916⅔, but by 1837 this was changed to .900 fine which continued until the end.

One Dollar Gold

The one dollar gold pieces were produced in three types—the last two thinner than the first and of larger diameter, obviously for simplified handling.

U.S. GOLD DOLLARS

Type 1: Liberty Head; smaller size, 1849–1854.

Type 2: Small Indian Head on larger diameter, 1854–1856.

Type 3: Larger Indian Head on diameter as above, 1856–1889.

Quarter Eagles ($2.50 Gold)

This denomination, a popular one when it was circulated, and now with collectors, was issued in two basic types through 1808. It was then reduced in diameter and given greater thickness. In 1840, a smaller head was instituted, similar to the larger coins of the period. The piece continued without essential change until 1907. The last type, the Indian Head, is notable in that its legends and main designs are *incuse* (indented rather than raised).

U.S. QUARTER EAGLES
($2.50 Gold)

Liberty capped; no stars on obverse, 1796.

Liberty capped with stars, 1796–1807.

Bust type, facing left; round cap.
    Large size, 1808.
    Reduced size, 1821–1834.

Liberty cap removed; no motto on reverse, 1834–1839.

Coronet, smaller head type, 1840–1907.

Indian head (incuse) type, 1908–1929.

Three Dollar Gold Pieces

These coins were unpopular with the public but nonetheless continued to be struck for about 35 years, though usually in comparatively small quantities. There was only one type, as shown.

Indian head, feathered headdress, 1854–1889.

Half Eagles (Five Dollars Gold)

This denomination was the first gold to be authorized and struck by the United States Mint. No mark of value was shown on the coins until 1807.

The 1822 Half Eagle is the most valuable of the regular gold coinage. There are many varieties in the earlier types, as usual.

U.S. HALF EAGLES
($5.00 Gold)

Capped Liberty; draped bust. Small, realistic eagle as well as heraldic eagle in same years, 1795 and 1796.

Similar, but all with heraldic eagle,   1797–1807.

Liberty, round cap; faces left. Mark of value 5D for first time, 1807–1812.

New type as above; but larger head, 1813–1828.

Smaller diameter, letters, dates and stars (not illustrated). 1829–1834.

No motto on reverse; reduced size, 1834–1838.

Coronet type. "In God We Trust" added to reverse within ribbon in 1866; 1839–1908.

Indian Head type (incuse as on $2.50 gold piece), 1908–1929.

Eagles (Ten Dollar Gold Pieces)

The early, larger diameter Eagles from 1795 through 1804 which had no mark of value, are magnificent examples of the finest in numismatic design. Unfortunately, they command very high prices and are beyond the reach of all but the wealthy.

When coinage of Eagles was resumed in 1838 with the Coronet type, they were of reduced weight and diameter and artistically far from the original pieces. In 1866, "In God We Trust" was added. When the lovely Indian Head type was designed by Augustus Saint-Gaudens, this motto was eliminated for the first year of issue because President Theodore Roosevelt objected to it. It was restored by Congress in time for the following year.

U.S. EAGLES
($10 gold pieces)

Capped bust; small, realistic eagle on reverse, 1795–1797.

Similar bust; heraldic eagle on reverse, 1797–1804.

Coronet type; no motto above eagle (not illustrated), 1838–1866. As above, but with motto added, 1866–1907.

Indian head type (no motto 1907 and part of 1908), 1907–1933.

Double Eagles (Twenty Dollar Gold Pieces)

These are the largest gold pieces issued by the U.S. for general circulation, weighing 516 grains, .900 fine—almost one troy ounce fine. The first type had the motto added in 1866 and "Twenty Dollars" was later spelled out. Earlier coins read "Twenty D."

The Saint-Gaudens type continued the great artistry of the Eagle he designed at the same period. In 1907, the year of issue, there was a high relief variety with the date in Roman numerals (MCMVII) as well as the regular issue in flat relief and the usual Arabic numerals. The high relief would not have been a practical coin for general circulation as it would have worn away too quickly. Therefore, the design was reworked.

U.S. DOUBLE EAGLES ($20 Gold Pieces)

Coronet type, 1849–1907. In 1866 the motto was added. TWENTY DOLLARS was spelled out in 1877.

St. Gaudens type (shown with and without motto on reverse), 1907–1932.

Privately Minted Gold Pieces

In the early years of the nineteenth century many gold coins circulated which were not sanctioned by the U.S. government, though at least condoned. Their production and use was a convenience to tradesmen and the general public, for regular mint issues were in exceedingly short supply. Besides, privately owned mints provided local facilities for newly mined gold, whether in the form of gold dust or nuggets, to be assayed, refined, and turned into handy coin of accepted standards of weight and fineness.

The first such mint was that of Templeton Reid in Lumpkin County, Georgia, who, in 1830, produced pieces equivalent to $2.50, five, and ten dollars. And in Rutherfordton, North Carolina, for a long period the source of most of this country's gold, the Bechtler Mint was set up about the same time. Besides issuing $2.50 and five dollar coins, the Bechtlers, who were metallurgists from Germany, struck the first one dollar gold piece which antedated the regular U.S. government series of this denomination.

With the opening up of the goldfields in California in 1849 and the consequent population explosion there and in other sections of the West, it was again urgent that newly mined gold be in the more convenient form of coin. A number of private mints opened in San Francisco before the branch mint was established there in 1854. The list was long, but Norris, Grieg & Norris of that city was first in 1849 with their Half Eagles. Moffat & Co. had the longest operation—from 1849 to 1853. Their gold ingots which were small rectangular slugs showing their name, weight, and purity, are numismatically famous, as are the five and ten dollar pieces they produced.

August Humbert was the assayer in San Francisco for the United States government. Before the regular mint went into operation there, he struck, among others, fifty dollar pieces in octagon shape which were accepted as legal tender by the Custom House, whereas gold dust, nuggets, and ordinary privately minted coins were not.

For smaller change, many California firms issued tiny 25 cent, 50 cent, and one dollar gold coins, both in octagon and round shape, from 1852 right up through 1882—by which time the U.S. government forbade the coinage of private money entirely.

Other series were produced in the cities and towns of Colorado, those of the Oregon Territory under authorization of its territorial legislature (later declared unconstitutional by the governor), and by the Mormons of Salt Lake City.

PRIVATE MINTS (GOLD)

$5 gold from the Bechtlers' private mint, Rutherfordton, Ga.

$16 ingot from Moffat & Co., San Francisco. Note that the fineness of the gold is shown as 20–3/4 carats, which works out to .865 fine. Regular U.S. gold coins were of .900 fineness.

$5 gold of Norris, Grieg & Norris, 1849. Thought to be the first of the California private gold coins.

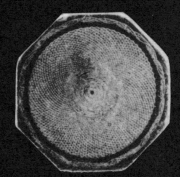

$50 octagonal gold issued by Moffat & Co., San Francisco in 1851. The U.S. Assayer, Augustus Humbert, added his name and the government stamp.

Moffat-Humbert/United States Assay Office, San Francisco, 1852. "Ten Dols."

Templeton Reid $5 and $2.50 gold pieces, issued in Gainesville, Ga.

$20 gold, Clark-Gruber (Denver) of 1860. Obverse shows Pike's Peak.

$10 gold piece of Oregon Exchange Co., Oregon City, dated 1849. These were known as Beaver coins from the design on the obverse.

Mormon $5 gold, Salt Lake City, 1849. Note the clasped hands on reverse, and obverse legend "Holiness to the Lord."

Commemorative Coins

Commemorative coins differ from medals in that they are always authorized by the government, and, most important, they may be freely circulated as currency at face value. However, few collectors would allow this to occur. Instead they would hold them in mint condition.

The ancient Greeks and Romans in effect struck commemorative coins to record important events at a time when their metal money, circulating over the known world, was perhaps the only means of mass communication between the ruler and his people. For several hundred years the modern nations have also issued commemorative coins. Some collectors specialize in marriage and coronation talers and crowns frequently struck in Europe during the past few centuries at least.

In our own country, the Columbian half dollar, initially struck in 1892, was the first commemorative coin of any denomination. In 1893, a silver quarter dollar bearing a portrait of Queen Isabella of Spain was issued at the request of the Board of Lady Governors of the Columbian Exposition that took place in Chicago. In 1900 came the Lafayette silver dollar, whose obverse shows the conjoined heads of both General Lafayette and George Washington.

No other commemorative silver dollars have been struck since, unless we count the "Peace" and Eisenhower issues which were originally conceived as commemoratives but were continued beyond the original years of issue as pieces for general circulation.

In 1903 the centenary of the Louisiana Purchase was honored by an issue of gold dollars in two varieties. These were followed by the Lewis and Clark Exposition gold dollars of 1904 and 1905 and other types later.

Quarter Eagles were issued for the Panama-Pacific Exposition of 1915 and the Philadelphia Sesquicentennial in 1926. The largest official coins the U.S. has ever struck were the two types of commemorative $50 gold pieces, also for the Panama-Pacific Exposition.

But it is the half dollars which make up the bulk of our commemorative series. Altogether there are 48 types, many of which were produced at the Denver and San Francisco mints as well as at Philadelphia.

All of these coins which commemorate special events or honor individuals were sold at a premium at the time of issue to raise money for the work of the planning authority involved. The Lafayette dollar went for two dollars, the difference going to the Lafayette Memorial Commission to help defray the expense of a monument to General Lafayette to be erected in Paris. This was to be an equestrian statue, similar to that shown on the reverse of the coin.

The last year of our commemorative coinage was 1954 and, in all probability, there will be no others. All of these pieces command a substantial premium from collectors. The Hawaiian Sesquicentennial issue of 1928 is valued highest among the silver half dollars. The fifty dollar round gold piece struck to commemorate the 1915 exposition, however, has been sold for $6,000. The prices of many others are far less astronomical.

U.S. COMMEMORATIVE COINS

Columbian Half Dollar, 1892–1893.

Isabella Quarter Dollar, 1893. About 24,000 were struck and sold at the time for one dollar each. It would cost about $100 now in uncirculated condition.

Lincoln-Illinois Centennial Half Dollar, 1918. The design of the Lincoln head was taken from the statue in Springfield, Ill.

Daniel Boone Bicentennial Half Dollar, 1934–1935. Boone's portrait on obverse; reverse shows him standing with Chief Black Fish.

Connecticut Tercentenary Half Dollar, 1935. The obverse shows the "Charter Oak" where the colony's charter was hidden during the reign of King James II who wanted to revoke it.

$50 gold piece, Panama-Pacific Exposition, 1915. Struck only at San Francisco, the design was by Robert Aitken. The same denomination was also issued in octagonal shape.

U.S. Grant Memorial
Gold Dollar, 1922.

Gold Dollar struck in 1904 and 1905 for the Lewis & Clark Centennial Exposition. Lewis is on the obverse, Clark on the reverse; an unusual departure in U.S. coinage.

Gold Dollars of the Louisiana Purchase Exposition, 1903. There were two types. Jefferson's head on one (left); President McKinley's on the other. They shared a common reverse.

Lafayette Silver Dollar, 1900. The equestrian statue of General Lafayette shown on the reverse was erected in Paris by gift of the American people. It was financed by the extra dollar charged for the coin—or at least in part, for only 36,000 were struck.

U.S. Proof and Special Mint Coins

Proofs, issued until 1968 by the Philadelphia mint and since then only by San Francisco, are specimen coins supplied for collectors. They are struck from polished dies which are replaced more frequently than those used for regular coins. The blanks are carefully selected and hand-fed into the slower-speed hydraulic presses, each being struck twice to bring up the detail of the design. The resulting pieces have sharper impressions than ordinary coins, and the surface takes on a shiny, mirrorlike quality. At various times proofs have also been given a sandblasted surface, producing a somewhat dull or matte finish.

Proof coins are also given special handling by the mint workers to avoid scratching, nicking, or other blemishes. Then they are packaged and sealed in presentation sets usually containing the cent, nickel, dime, quarter, and half dollar. The initial Eisenhower proof dollars were packaged individually in rather elaborate slipcases.

Special mint coins are regular production coins, but selected from the first strikings off the dies (thus sharper and more brilliant) and have been made available mainly during the years when no proofs were struck, as in 1965, 1966, and 1967. These are also mint packaged.

The Mint has always charged a premium over and above the value of the coins themselves for both proof and mint sets. They may be purchased direct in the year of issue.

Proof coins are avidly collected and valuations have risen considerably over the years from their issue prices. Invariably, collectors retain them in the original mint packaging, never touching the coins, to keep them unimpaired.

Proof coins were struck even in the early decades of the nineteenth century, and, of course, these old ones are extremely rare. They were generally issued for presentation to government officials or foreign dignitaries in those times gone by and were not easily come by so far as the rank-and-file collector was concerned. The modern period of proof coins in the U.S. may be considered to be from about 1860.

Proofs were discontinued in 1916, resumed in 1936, dropped again during the war years through 1949, and then production was started once more. There was a further lapse after 1964. They are now available again and probably will continue year by year, barring a crisis. Certainly the Treasury Department has discovered how enormously profitable such sales to collectors really are. The Eisenhower proof dollars, for example, reap a veritable harvest for the government.

In this sense, however, the U.S. may have woken up late. A great many of the new small countries have been issuing proof sets of their coins to collectors at unconscionable prices for a long time.

As for the collecting aspect of proof coins, there are two schools of thought among the numismatic fraternity. Some love them, and others feel their collections do not need to include them. They look upon proofs as souvenirs, since they are not actual production pieces designed to circulate and thus further the economy of the country, not just the Treasury! But you must be the judge of this yourself. Beyond a doubt these brilliant pieces are quite handsome.

A good way to display and protect proof or mint sets.
(Photo courtesy of Whitman Coin Products.)

Foreign Coins That Were Once Legal Tender in the U.S.

Even though the U.S. Mint was established in 1792, its production fell far below the normal "hard money" requirements of trade. Thus, as late as 1857 foreign coins passed as legal tender in the United States to compensate.

The famous Spanish milled dollar, also known as the Pillar dollar because of the representation of the pillars of Hercules on the reverse, was very well liked both before and after the Revolution and, in fact, was the chief coin of the colonists when obtainable. The "Piece of Eight" of pirate fame was a coin valued at eight reales and became the basis for our own dollar. Two reales were thus worth a quarter in our money, and it is said that sometimes the coin was cut into four segments for smaller change. Hence our expression "two bits."

It was a bewildering confusion of foreign currency that must have passed through merchants' and bank tellers' hands in those days: the silver dollars of Spain, Mexico, Peru, Chile; French écus and five franc pieces; English crowns, and many others. Then there were the gold pieces: Spanish doubloons and pistoles, French Louis d'ors, Portuguese moidores, English guineas, and so on. In addition to these were the fractions and multiples of the coins mentioned, in both metals. Small wonder that anyone who handled money at the time needed a set of jeweler's scales on his counter to weigh doubtful coin.

Compounding the money shortage caused by the fact that the United States simply did not coin enough money at the time, very early in the nineteenth century it was found that Congress had established an unrealistic relationship between gold and silver. Coin of these metals were often exported to countries abroad, where they were worth more as bullion than as money here. When the ratio was finally changed and the weights of our coins were reduced, the situation improved to a marked degree.

This was in accordance with the rules of "intrinsic value." Ever since the beginnings of coinage, emphasis had been placed on the weight and fineness of a nation's money. It had to be of an acceptable standard. If coins were overweight or over-fine in terms of the market price for bullion, it meant that the public would remove them from circulation. Actually to maintain the precise balance in terms of relative values of silver to gold and coin these metals according to it was eventually discovered to be an impossibility.

"Bimetallism" finally ceased to have a place in our economy. Gold was to reign supreme without regard to the price of silver. Though in 1933 gold coin and gold certificates were withdrawn from circulation, gold alone among the metals remained the basis for our currency and those of the rest of the world.

Silver coins before the mid-1800's became "subsidiary" money. That is, their silver content was worth less than face value. Therefore, it was to no one's interest to melt down or export them as bullion. In this sense the situation recently changed. Our silver coins became worth more than "face" when the price of silver skyrocketed on the free market. That is why, since 1965, we have had our "clad" coins of little intrinsic value.

FOREIGN COINS THAT WERE ONCE LEGAL TENDER IN THE U.S.

"Pillar" Dollar; Spain, 8 reales, 1761.

Mexico, 8 reales, 1805; Carlos IV.

Mexico, one-half reale, 1810; Ferdinand VI.

But nowadays it doesn't matter an iota what money is made of (except, perhaps, to die-hard numismatists). The trend for general circulation is away from precious metals entirely. Money today is valued by the backing of sufficient reserves held by a strong government. You will accept U.S. coins of nickel, copper, or plastic, for that matter, if they are ever issued in that material, just as readily as you once did when our coinage contained its full complement of silver, .900 fine.

A collection of U.S. coins should be rounded out by specimens of some of the foreign coins that used to be current here so many years ago, for they have great historical interest.

Spain, 4 Escudos (gold) 1708; Philip V.

Great Britain, Double sovereign   (gold)   1823; George IV.

Great   Britain,   "Spade" Guinea   (gold)   1787; George III.

France, Ecu, 1716; Louis XV.

Great Britain, Half sovereign (gold) 1817; George III.

Portugal, 400 reis, 1768; Jose I.

France, piece of 6 livres, 1793 (Year 2 of the Republic).

Siege Pieces, Money of Necessity, Countermarked, and Overstruck Coins

An interesting area of specialization may be found in collecting siege pieces, necessity money, and countermarked and overstruck coins.

As the name implies, *siege pieces* are emergency money issued during the time of siege, either of a city or stronghold, designed to pay troops and for provisions and other expenses required by a beleaguered army, and generally to act as a medium of exchange. Often these pieces were rudely cut in oddly shaped metal blanks and are distinguished by a mark of value and the name or arms of the place of issue. There may be considerable elaboration but this would depend upon whether proper coining tools had been available.

Siege pieces of the early times were usually struck in acceptable gold or silver and valued accordingly, though others were done in copper. The silver and gold might have belonged originally to the burghers or nobles of the area in the form of trenchers, bowls, or plates. Many of the old siege pieces were marked "OBS" for *obsidional,* the Latin for besieged. Since Europe was constantly at war, particularly up to the end of the eighteenth and into the nineteenth centuries, many such pieces exist.

Money of necessity is similar to the above in the sense that it is not a regular issue. For one reason or another, the governing authority during a state of emergency did not have the means to supply normal coinage. A revolutionary or provisional government might have struck such pieces. As we shall see later, "tokens" fall into this classification as well.

Nowadays metal siege and necessity pieces would probably be superseded by issues of paper currency—promises to pay, whether worth anything or not. The Continental currency issued by the Continental Congress during the Revolution would fall into this

103

category, as do the "Assignats" of the French Revolution.

Coins of other nations have at various times been *countermarked* by governments to authorize their use as legal tender within a jurisdiction. They would supplement a national or colonial currency if in short supply. And sometimes such countermarked coins have been the *only* currency of a country. The countermarks as a rule are stamped on the obverse of the coin in some small design, occasionally with the accepted valuation.

Typical of countermarked coins once used in England are eight and four reale pieces—the Spanish and Mexican milled dollar and its half. The countermark was a small head of the reigning King George III (1760–1820), actually the one that was used as the hallmark on sterling silver of the period. The reason for these emergency pieces was that regular issues of silver coins were not being struck by the Royal Mint and coins of those denominations were sorely needed.

Overstruck coins are those which are first annealed to soften them, and then struck again with entirely different dies, obliterating the original design. The original coins could have been from some other country, perhaps received as booty during a war, or simply obtained by purchase. On the other hand, Imperial Russia frequently overstruck its own coins with new designs during the eighteenth century. These overstruck pieces often show parts of the original design.

SIEGE PIECES, MONEY OF NECESSITY, COUNTERMARKED, AND OVERSTRUCK COINS

Klippe Taler (undated); city of Emden, Germany during reign of Emperor Ferdinand II (1619–1637).

Newark, England; 30 pence or half-crown, 1646.
Struck by forces of Charles I during the civil war.

Coin Struck in 1641 during
the siege of Artois, France.

12-½ stuivers issued at Groningen, Netherlands, when besieged by Spanish (uniface).

Spanish dollar (8 reales) of 1802 and France cou-
ronne of 1767 both countermarked with the head of
George III. These drew the sarcastic comment "Two
Kings" heads not worth a crown" for they were underweight in relation to the English piece of 5 shillings for
which they passed current.

Primitive, Commodity, and Curious Money

Long before the advent of coined money, there were mediums of exchange in every civilization. Gold and silver bullion were, of course, always valued highly. The ancient *talent,* for example, was both a weight and a monetary unit whose value varied with time and place. The *shekel* of Biblical fame was also a unit of weight among the Phoenicians, Hebrews, and others long before it became a coin.

The Chinese, when they began to move out of the barter period about the seventh to the fourth century B.C. had a series of knife and spade money which was cast from bronze and based on the shapes of the objects once used for barter. Much more recently tea bricks have passed as money in China as well as in Siberia.

Sweden, about the year 1715, issued what was probably the most inconvenient currency in modern times. This was the huge copper plate money of which some pieces weighed as much as 45 lbs. They were marked with the intrinsic value of the metal contained in them. Perhaps you have already heard of the stone money—tremendous wheels of stone—once used by the natives of the Island of Yap in the western Pacific.

The Aztecs of Mexico, before the conquest by Spain, used chocolate as their currency, with cocoa beans as the small change of the people. Along with these, T-shaped pieces of copper as well as gold dust passed as money—the latter conveniently packaged in the hollow of bird quills and standardized according to the size of the quills.

In North America, the beaver skin was so generally accepted by the Indians as a medium of exchange that the colonists also adopted this as a form of money. In the far north, where the beaver was unknown, the Eskimos used the skins of the land otter and the large hair seal.

The wampum of legend, called *peage* by the Indians of the Atlantic seaboard, which also found its way into the interior, was generally fashioned from clam shells into oblong beads about a quarter inch long and half as much in diameter. There was a regular rate of exchange. In the year 1640, white wampum went at four to the penny, while blue was worth twice as much. Later, wampum depreciated so that it was accepted at only six to the penny. By the end of the seventeenth century, wampum, always worthless in Europe, became unacceptable even to the colonists. Tobacco and beaver skins, however, remained as standards of trade on both sides of the Atlantic.

Lastly, we must not forget that handmade nails, most important in a young colony where hard currency was practically non-existent, passed as currency in the early days of New England.

PRIMITIVE, COMMODITY AND CURIOUS MONEY

African Shell money.

West African Ring money. (The ancient Celts had a similar currency.)

Stone money (holed); African Gold Coast/ Togo.

Ancient China: Hollow handled Spade money (c. 600 B.C.).

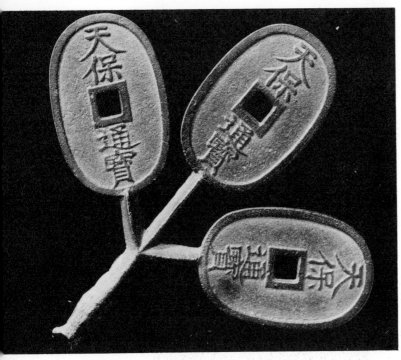

Japanese money in form of a tree, c. 1835 A.D.

Chinese Knife money, first century A.D.

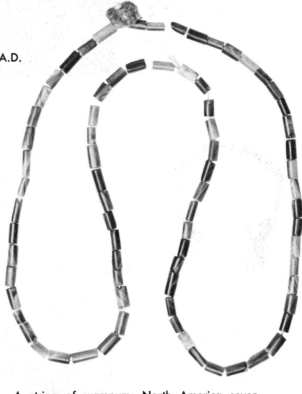

A string of wampum; North America seventeenth century.

Tokens

We have seen how money remained in short supply both in colonial America and up to the time the U.S. Mint was placed in operation, and how private firms or individuals attempted to cope with the situation. But long after the United States had a national currency of its own, the supply of coin was still never plentiful, even with the addition of the foreign coins which passed as legal tender.

It does seem unthinkable that in modern times one may have the resources to pay for something, however small, yet find it impossible to complete the purchase because regular coins have disappeared from circulation. However, serious shortages of minor pieces have occurred in this country as recently as 1964. Hoarding has been the major cause.

There was plenty of precedent in the nineteenth century for private enterprise to fill the lack of coins with tokens—stamped pieces of metal which pass as currency in excess of their intrinsic value.

During the period 1834–1844, when coin shortages became particularly acute, what came to be called "Jackson" or "Hard Times" tokens were privately issued. Usually of copper in the size of the large cents of the time, the pieces came in two types: those with political and satirical messages concerned with President Jackson's running feud with the United States Bank, and straight "Merchants' Tokens," also known as "Storecards." Both were gratefully accepted in change by the public. Several hundred different Jackson tokens exist.

During the Civil War, U.S. cents were again hoarded, and to substitute for them there was a huge private emission of "Civil War Tokens" arbitrarily valued at one cent. Many of these advertised merchants' wares while others contained patriotic or political designs and inscriptions and carried no advertising. Over 10,000 varieties exist. The latter pieces were supplied for general circulation by various manufacturers, who indeed "turned a pretty penny" in more ways than one. These tokens, the size of our current cent, cost only a fraction of a cent to produce. They served their purpose well, but since they bore no indication of their origin, no one was to have the eventual responsibility for redeeming them when the regular U.S. coinage returned.

Among the Civil War issues were the "Sutlers' Tokens." Sutlers were licensed to follow the armies with wagons well stocked with food, liquor, and whatever else soldiers might wish to buy. Thus they acted as a sort of private forerunner of the PX store.

It is interesting as a sidelight to know that because the lightweight tokens of the Civil War period had proved so acceptable to the public, they actually paved the way for the government issue of the small bronze cents introduced in 1864. These slim pieces, having the same dimensions as the present cent, were struck at the reduced weight of 48 grains. The original small bronze cents first coined in 1859 weighed 72 grains, the difference being that they were much thicker.

The United States government itself issued a series of tokens in 1935. These were for the Alaska Rural Rehabilitation Corporation and were used by the settlers of the Matanuska Valley Project for about six months. Eight denominations of these "Bingles," as they were called, were available from one cent to ten dollars. All were later recalled and redeemed for regular U.S. currency, except those that fell into collectors' hands.

Merchants' tokens were issued extensively in Great Britain, particularly during the eighteenth and early nineteenth centuries, as that country was consistently plagued with shortages of minor coins. Even as early as the reign of Queen Elizabeth I (1558–1603) no halfpennies and farthings were obtainable because it was too costly to produce such small silver pieces. The value of the metal had increased so sharply that such coins would have had to be heavily debased with copper or made much smaller, and thus impractical to handle.

The English Queen was aware of earlier problems caused by a debased coinage and therefore refused to sanction a return to it in even a minor way. The immediate problem was solved in a roundabout manner. For a farthing's purchase you handed over a penny, receiving the three-farthing piece as change. A halfpenny purchase worked similarly, except that you paid twopence and got back a three-half-penny piece. However, in the reign of James I (1603–1625) the coinage of copper farthing tokens was licensed for the first time. But shortages of small-value coins continued in England for the next two centuries for one reason or another, and merchants' tokens became the answer to the problem.

The issuance of tokens in both the United States and Great Britain is now illegal, and the laws are enforced. You may remember our most recent coin shortage, which occurred in 1964 and resulted from the well-founded rumors that the silver in our coins would be removed. Consequently, silver coins were hoarded. At that time the Treasury Department refused to allow a grocery chain to ease the situation by issuing scrip. That company and others in a similar quandary were thus forced to drop any such idea. In fact, it is no longer within the law even for towns to circulate wooden nickels or token pieces of any kind for general circulation to celebrate, say, a centennial year.

In 1929, Martin Coles Harman, a British subject who happened to own the whole of Lundy Island off the coast of England in the Bristol Channel, evidently felt his ownership gave him the sovereign right to coinage. He had two handsome pieces struck with his likeness on the obverse. The reverses bore the puffin, a bird that often nests on the island. These puffin and half-puffin pieces circulated on the island for a short time but finally had to be withdrawn. Mr. Harman was subjected to a fine by the British court for violation of the coinage act, payable in English pounds—not puffins. His pieces, however, now command a large premium from collectors.

In the early days of the sales tax in the United States, tokens were issued by state and local governments to facilitate making exact change on purchases where the tax amounted to less than a cent. These have since disappeared from use, as such taxes are now averaged out to the next cent. They were made of plastic, light metal, and even cardboard.

On an everyday basis, "Transportation Tokens" are still with us. Then there have been "Public Telephone Tokens," apparently never in widespread use, but supplied in sections of certain cities where coin boxes might habitually be pilfered. And for years, those who had to trade at company stores in many factory towns were usually given all or part of their wages in "Company Tokens" instead of actual currency, and were expected to spend them at these stores.

So you see how many different kinds of tokens there have been; obviously, far more than have been mentioned here. But tokens generally belong rightfully in three broad categories. These are the necessity pieces issued because of actual shortage of official money; convenience tokens, such as transportation issues and the like; and straight advertising pieces which never were intended to pass as money at all, but were used for promotions—commercial, political, patriotic, or private. Then it is possible to stretch the point a bit and call the private or territorial gold coins "tokens" because they too were issued to alleviate shortages of gold coin in the local pioneer areas. However, they were generally equivalent in fineness and weight to the national money, which, strictly speaking, should automatically take them out of the token class.

Whatever one may call them, tokens are interesting pieces of nostalgia and have played a part in the country's history. All are collectible and collected, in many instances most avidly. Certainly, well-balanced collections of this nation's coinage should include examples of the "Hard Times" and Civil War tokens, since they did circulate freely as money, although unauthorized. There are many specialist collectors within any given series. Fortunately many of the tokens can be acquired for nominal sums.

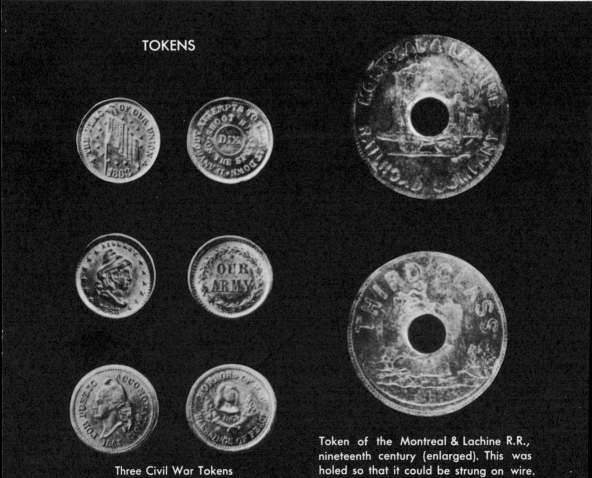

TOKENS

Three Civil War Tokens

Token of the Montreal & Lachine R.R., nineteenth century (enlarged). This was holed so that it could be strung on wire.

Mexican christening
token,1886 (enlarged).

Great Britain: Harman/Lundy
Island "Puffin" of 1929.

Great Britain: Eighteenth century Merchant tokens which passed at a halfpenny.

Three "Hard Times" tokens of the 1830's used as a medium of exchange instead of the hard-to-come by U.S. government issue of large cents.

CIVIL WAR TOKENS

1863 Kerr sutler token

Above, an Aaron White token of New Boston, Conn.
White was the leading coin hoarder of Civil War.

Dix Civil War token

Jefferson Davis Civil War token

Abraham Lincoln Civil War token

Indiana merchants issued store cards, such as
two above and below, which circulated as cents.

War-Peace Civil War token

Monitor Civil War token

Paper Money

Much earlier we have said that the term "numismatics" also includes paper money, a highly specialized field by itself and to be touched upon only lightly here.

The honor of inventing paper money belongs to China, where some form of paper currency was in use prior to 618 A.D. There is still extant in the library of Columbia University a bronze block for printing Chinese notes at the time of Kublai Khan (about 1287 A.D.). It was not until 1661 that the first paper money got its start in Europe—"Bearer" notes issued by the Bank of Sweden. Similar notes were issued by the Bank of England thirty years later. These were copper engraved and actually promised to pay on demand a specified sum to a named recipient or "Bearer." Space for this was left blank, to be filled in at time of issuance. The notes were numbered and signed by hand.

Paper currency in America was issued by the original colonies, counties, cities, banks, and individuals from about 1690 to 1776. It bulked very importantly in the economy of the times because, as we have seen, so little hard currency circulated. At the time of the Revolution, the Continental Congress authorized its issues of "Continental Currency" which was expected to be redeemed in the equivalent of Spanish milled dollars or in gold or silver bullion. However, we know how its value sank so low that the expression "not worth a Continental" entered the language. Before the Federal government was established, the various states emitted their own issues, a right which was of course denied them later under the Constitution.

In the early nineteenth century, banks throughout the United States issued their own paper currency and much of it ended up as worthless because many of them were forced to suspend payments in specie. While there was a small issue of interest-bearing U.S. Treasury notes about 1815, which were redeemed quickly, the United States notes (greenbacks) of 1861 were the first of the government issues. They were to help finance the Civil War, and went into general circulation. National Bank notes, gold and silver certificates, and Federal Reserve notes have all played their part in the economy of our country. At present, of course, only the Federal Reserve notes are current, all others having been withdrawn from circulation.

Note collectors thus have a wealth of material to draw upon, U.S. and foreign. Some concentrate on the "Broken Bank" notes—those issued by banks that went out of business, bankrupt or otherwise, and whose paper was in many instances heavily ornamented with carefully engraved vignettes and other decorations. They are highly valued now by collectors. Others find special interest in the early paper money of America, or perhaps concentrate upon printing errors in the modern currency, of which, surprisingly, many turn up on the market.

Paper money, through the few centuries it has been in existence, has taken many proportions and sizes. The present series is much smaller than, though proportionally the same as, those prior to 1930. Paper money is to be found printed and lithographed as well as engraved, on a single side as well as both, and in one or many colors. In our own country during the Civil War we had fractional currency (denominations below one dollar). Some of the National Bank notes have been for odd denominations, such as for three and eight dollars.

Chinese block-printed note on bark of the fourteenth century, for one Kuan (100 cash). Size about 6″ x 9″. The face side is shown.

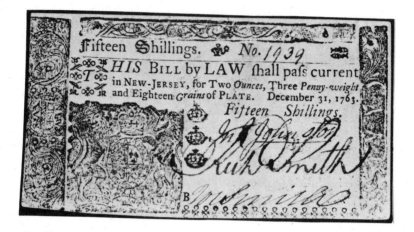

Fifteen shilling note, New Jersey, 1763. This was redeemable either for the face amount, or the equivalent in "plate" which would work out to 1050 grains of silver .925 fine—a total of 70 grains per shilling.

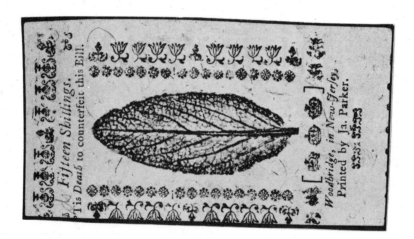

Six shilling note, Delaware, dated January 1, 1776. See the legend "To counterfeit is Death" as on a number of issues of the period.

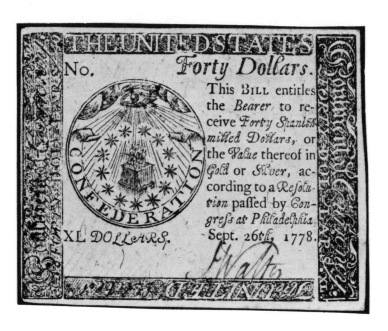

Forty dollar note of the Continental Congress, 1778.

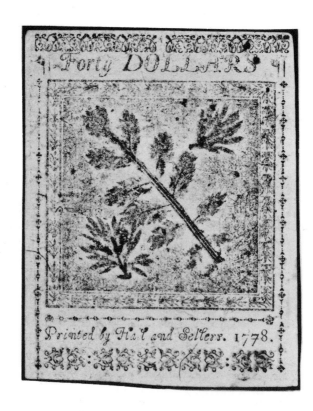

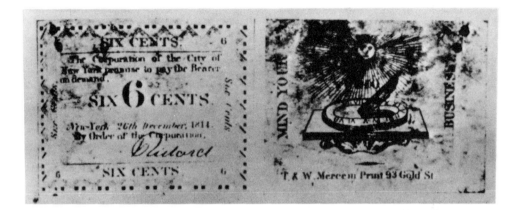

Six cent note of New York City, 1814. "Mind Your Business" appeared on the pattern Continental Dollar and the Fugio cent and was taken from these coins.

A "Broken Banknote" for one dollar, issued by the City Bank of Leavenworth, Kansas, 1856. It was not backed by specie but still a convenience when hard money was unobtainable.

Fractional currency of the U.S. government during and after the Civil War which served as small change. Still redeemable, but much more valuable numismatically.

Encased postage stamps, 1862. The patented brass
frame protected the stamps and permitted them to
circulate freely as currency. The reverse carried advertising legends.

Five pound note of the Bank of England dated 1818. As on
all early currency, this was hand signed. Face side shown.

Medals

Medals are usually round but occasionally they are rectangular, oval, or some other shape. Most often you will find them carrying both obverse and reverse designs, but sometimes they may be uniface.

The earliest medals were produced by the Greeks and Romans, those of the latter being notable for their realistic portraiture. Actually they were medallic coins, as the illustrations show. A great revival of medallic art took place during the Renaissance period in Italy and then swept Europe. Many of the finest artists, including Benvenuto Cellini and Albrecht Dürer, designed exquisite medals. Originally all of them were cast, but with the invention of improved machinery they were later struck from dies, as are most of those designed in modern times.

High relief is usually a feature of the medal and a great deal more detail is possible than can be obtained on a coin. Slower presses are used for their production and the best are struck several times, each strike bringing up more of the detail. In these they differ from coin production, which naturally requires high volume and wears the dies faster, often resulting in weak strikes. Coins also have lower relief and less detail to ensure minimal wear in circulation and must be stackable for commercial use.

During the fifteenth and sixteenth centuries a nobleman's or gentleman's dress was not considered complete unless he wore a medal suspended from a heavy chain around his neck. We seem to be seeing a revival of this now.

As far back as our Continental Congress, medals were authorized by that body to be struck in France at the Paris Mint to commemorate the heroes of the Revolutionary War.

There are several categories of medals. *Commemorative medals* are issued to honor a notable person or call attention to some event past, present, or future. *Civil or military medals and decorations* are awarded by governments, orders, or private organizations and institutions and can be for heroism, service, or distinction of one kind or another. And of course *religious medals* are well known. Then there are the *art medals*, which owe their existence to none of the above reasons but are frequently very handsome in their own right. In the nineteenth century, France became a leader in the design and production of art medals of great distinction.

Medal collecting is being taken up by an increasingly large group in this country and elsewhere and you can find excellent examples of medallic art on just about any subject that interests you. To name only a few: those on some phase of, or personality in, Science, Industry, Business, Military, Medicine, Art, Music, the Stage, Literature, Statesmanship, and Aviation.

Military medals and decorations as well as foreign *orders of knighthood* are a special study in themselves. Physically their form may take the shape of a disc, cross, or star, and they are frequently attached to their own distinctive ribbons. If you decide to specialize in any of these, it would be best first to read the extensive literature available on them to give you proper background and perspective.

Nowadays there has been a vast outpouring of commemorative medals from many sources struck in bronze, silver, and occasionally gold or other metals, precious or not. The U.S. Mint at Philadelphia has had the responsibility for the design and striking of the official Presidential inaugural medals, although at times private medallic firms may help to produce them. The U.S. Mint has also issued its famous Indian Peace series and other medals from time to time in varying degrees of artistry, which are available to the public. It is possible to obtain medals of the great Americans elected to the Hall of Fame in New York, including many of the older ones, by contacting that institution. The U.S. Mint will send literature on the subjects it still has for sale. Some coin dealers carry medals of various kinds in stock or list them in their catalogs.

Modern medals range from artistically excellent to terrible. It is unfortunate that too many of them, lacking most elements of good design and even taste, are rushed through production to capitalize on current events and an awakened public appetite for medallic "art." Sometimes it seems that almost every firm equipped with a stamping press is ready and willing to jump into the act. For example, of the vast variety of medals struck to commemorate the first moon landing, or to honor President Kennedy after the assassination, most were simply awful.

Again, in the last few years the public has been bombarded by advertisements, in the press and through the mails, of series after series of newly issued commemoratives. These are usually represented as heirloom items, with the implication that after you buy them they will steadily increase in value. This is because they are issued in limited, numbered sets or pieces. Also, since most of the medals in this class are struck not only in sterling (.925) silver but in the almost pure (.999) silver, one of the claims is that their high intrinsic value is something to fall back on.

The reader is reminded that the silver content of such medals in relation to the original purchase price is quite low, as anyone who cares to take the trouble to weigh them on a jeweler's scale can quickly ascertain. As for "heirloom" value, this remains to be seen in the next generation or two or three. While the manufacturers do create artificial scarcity by limiting the editions, nonetheless they seem to be limited only by the numbers the makers believe they can sell. It is, of course, entirely possible that the mechanical counter attached to the press can conveniently get out of order. Thus it is doubtful that the present crop of commemorative medals emanating from the private mints is a good "investment" as such, however desirable they may be otherwise.

So a word of caution. If medallic art interests you enough to form a collection, let it be on some other basis than appreciation of the dollars you may put into it. Be selective in what you buy, passing up the examples which have no merit. For these have no place in a serious collector's cabinet, unless you wish to start an "atrocity corner" for the fun of it.

MEDALS

Medallic silver decadrachm of Syracuse, Sicily by Euainetos, beginning of fourth century B.C. This large piece might have been given as an award at Olympic games.

Roman Empire: Constantius
I (Flavius Valerius Constantius, 293–306); gold,
struck to commemorate his
entry into London.

Italian Renaissance: Medal of Leo-
nello, Duke of Este (1397–1455).
Designed by Antolio Pisano, called
Pisanello.

Alexander Graham Bell's medal in the Hall of Fame series.

Benjamin Franklin medal

Andrew Johnson Indian Peace medal.

George Washington Indian Peace medal.

Lyndon Johnson
Presidential Scholar medal.

President Joseph A. Garfield memorial medal.

A Short Glossary of Numismatic Terms

ALLOY: A mixture of metals, precious, base, or both.

ALTERED DATE: A coin's date changed to a rarer one, usually by tooling, with intent to defraud collectors.

ASSAY COMMISSION: A group of citizens appointed annually to check on the weights and fineness of U.S. coins produced at the mints; now purely honorary and routine. An outgrowth of Britain's ancient "Trial of the Pyx." In medieval times, sample coins were placed in boxes and examined, and severe penalties were suffered if the discrepancy was too great.

ATTRIBUTION: When we attribute a coin we assign it to its place in history. With a coin of the Roman Empire, this would include the emperor's name, year of striking, place of minting, value, etc.

BAG MARKS: The nicks, scratches, and imperfections in new coins that may result from being placed in bags for handling.

BILLON: Silver which has been heavily alloyed with more than its weight of base metal.

BLANKS: See *planchet.*

BRACTEATES: Very thin medieval coins of the twelfth to fourteenth century, which originated in Germany and are considered to have had the value of the denar, or silver penny. The obverse designs were stamped through a foil of metal, usually silver, and accordingly showed up intaglio on the reverse. Diameter was as much as 1½".

BROCKAGE: From "break" or "broken." An imperfectly minted coin. They do slip through the modern mints.

BRONZE: An alloy chiefly of copper and tin.

CARTOUCHE: An oval or scroll-shaped panel containing an inscription or ornamentation.

CAST COINS: Coins made by pouring molten metal into a mold, as opposed to those struck from dies. The old Chinese "cash" are convenient examples of this method.

130

CHOPMARK: As *countermark*. Practiced by Chinese merchants to attest the purity of Spanish or Mexican dollars, U.S. Trade dollars, etc.

CLAD COINAGE: "Sandwich" metal of which U.S. coins are now made. Contains an inner core of pure copper bonded to outer layers of copper-nickel (or silver).

COB: Actually this means "Lump" and refers to old Spanish silver and gold pieces of the seventeenth and eighteenth centuries which were rudely hewn from larger cast ingots to the value of so many reales or escudos, then stamped with dies into rough coins for convenient transport from the new world to Europe. "Pirate gold."

COUNTERMARK: In effect a "hallmark" to indicate that a coin of a foreign country is acceptable as a medium of exchange elsewhere. Private merchants have also countermarked coins, both in the East and West.

COUNTERSTAMP: See *countermark*.

CUT MONEY: Segments cut from larger silver pieces, usually the Spanish milled dollar, to provide small change. Practiced by the colonial governments of the British West Indies in eighteenth and early nineteenth centuries and elsewhere.

DOUBLOON: A famous Spanish and Spanish-American gold coin issued into the nineteenth century and worth 16 U.S. silver dollars at the time. Also called the gold "onza" or ounce.

DUCAT: A gold coin of Europe first issued by Roger of Sicily about 1150. There are also silver ducats.

EDGE: The extreme border of a coin or medal, whose thickness is either left plain, as on U.S. cents or nickels; reeded, as on dimes, etc.; or edge-marked with lettering.

ELECTRUM: A natural pale yellow alloy of gold and silver. Used by the Greeks in early times in its natural state for coinage.

ENCASED POSTAGE STAMPS: During a period of the Civil War coin shortage, postage stamps were used as small change, but very inconveniently. Patented brass frames were developed and the stamps were slipped into these, to be viewed through thin sheets of mica. The reverse carried an advertisement.

ENGRAILED EDGE: Indenting at the edge of a coin with small concave curves, border, or a ring of dots.

EXERGUE: The segment beneath the base line of a coin or medal; often this space will include the date.

FIELD: The surface of a coin or medal not occupied by the main device or inscription.

FLAN: See *planchet*.

FLORIN: Originally a gold piece struck in the city-state of Florence in 1252 and widely imitated in Europe. Also struck in silver. The name is still used in Europe for some modern pieces.

GREENBACKS: Legal tender, non-interest bearing notes of the U.S. first issued as a Civil War measure in 1862. The devices were printed with green ink.

HAMMERED COINS: Those struck by hand with a hammer; used through the seventeenth century and occasionally much later.

HOLING (HOLED): A coin or medal with a hole punched in it, usually so that it could be ribboned, is said to be "holed." Never do this to a coin or medal you treasure. Of course some pieces are actually issued that way, but for different reasons, as a rule.

INCUSE: The main device and/or legend impressed into the planchet instead of raised in the usual relief. The last U.S. $2.50 and five dollar gold pieces are excellent examples of incuse work.

INITIAL MARK (i.m.): Sometimes used to denote a cross or other symbol at the beginning of the legend on both sides of an old coin. Often helpful in assigning the approximate period of issue of early, undated pieces. This is a term often confused with "mint mark."

INSCRIPTION: Usually the horizontal text on a coin or medal.

KEY DATE COINS: Rare dates and mint marks within a series.

KLIPPE MONEY: A coin struck on a square or diamond shaped planchet. Means "to clip," or "cut."

LEGEND: Inscription, motto, or title, especially one surrounding the field or placed on a heraldic shield.

LETTERED EDGE: Lettering that appears around the edge of a coin or medal.

LOZENGE SHAPE: Diamond shape. A heraldic term.

MARK OF VALUE: The value at which a coin is tariffed by the issuing government, now usually shown on the reverse. In early times there was no indication of this on the coin at all.

MILLED COINS: Originally used to describe coins struck by machinery or "mills," such as the Spanish milled dollars. The first milled coins were produced in limited quantity in the sixteenth century.

MILLING: To make indentations in the rim of a coin, causing ridges to appear on the face. Wrongly used to describe "reeding" at the edge.

MINT MARK: A letter or symbol on a coin to indicate the mint that produced it.

MINOR COINS: Coins valued below the dollar or other monetary unit. The fractions.

MINT LUSTRE: The original high lustre of a piece as it came from the mint.

MULE: A transitional coin whose obverse and reverse designs are not compatible in that the characteristics of one of the dies used would be of an earlier period than those of the other.

OBSIDIONAL COIN: A siege piece, issued within a city or stronghold during time of siege to pay troops, etc.

OBVERSE: The front side or "heads." Bears the principal portrait or inscription. In coins of the U.S., the side bearing the date, irrespective of the device. Many foreign coins do not have portraits.

ORICHALCUM: Brass alloyed with zinc. The Roman coinage includes much of this material.

OVERDATE: The correction of older dies at the mint to bring them up to date, as, for example, the 1869 cent wherein the 9 appears struck over the 8. This does not occur very often, but when it does, we have another variety.

OVERSTRIKE: To impress an existing coin with a completely new design, so as to change all elements.

OXIDATION: Occasional blackening of a silver piece, the result of chemical reaction. If this happens, leave it as is.

PATINA: A film formed on copper and bronze, usually by exposure to the elements. Natural patinas of varying shades of green have artistic and numismatic appeal.

PATTERN PIECE: This is an actual specimen of a proposed coin, usually complete in every respect, but minted before authorization as currency. Some existing patterns of accepted coins are exactly as those later produced; others vary. Patterns are often struck in several metals.

PEDIGREE: Since many rare coins have been in famous collections and cataloged, these individual pieces are considered to have "pedigrees." If you acquire such pieces it is desirable to retain whatever information has been passed on.

PLANCHET: A blank disk of metal (or possibly some other shape) ready to be stamped as a coin or medal. Same as *blank* or *flan*.

PROOF COIN: A coin struck from a specially treated die on selected planchets, having greater sharpness of impression than those intended for circulation, and usually a mirror finish. Proofs are sometimes struck in metals of higher or lower value than those of regular issues.

PROVENANCE: Origin or source. If a coin is known to have come from a certain hoard, that would be its provenance.

REEDING: The fine grooves or knurling on the edges of dimes, quarters, half dollars, etc.

RELIEF: The projection of figures, portraiture, etc., from the background. Modern coins are said to be in very low relief; medals as a rule are in considerably higher relief.

RESTRIKE: A coin of earlier date, struck again considerably later, as a rule, for special purposes, such as to fill the wants of collectors. This is happening in certain European countries right now, and the collector should beware that the "rare" coin he is offered to complete his series is really freshly minted and not rare at all.

REVERSE: The back or "tails."

RIM: The raised or projecting edge or border of a coin or medal.

SPECIE: Coin, or hard money, usually of gold or silver; as in "specie payment" in exchange for paper money. All one can get now is more paper currency.

STOPS: Small dots, crosses, stars, or some other device used to divide words, almost always found on coins of the eighteenth century and before. But see the reverse of the U.S. Peace dollar. Not to be confused with groupings or clusters which may be part of a design.

STRIATIONS: Minute parallel grooves or lines.

STRIKE: The sharpness or lack of it in a coin. We say, "It is a good strike." On the other hand, the English say, "Well struck up."

TETRADRACHM: An ancient Greek or Egyptian coin or others of the period, valued at four drachmas. About the size of a modern quarter, but much thicker and heavier. Most of them are very handsome.

TONING: An iridescence that sometimes forms on the surface of a silver coin or medal. Colors may be predominantly bluish, greenish, reddish. Highly prized numismatically.

TRIAL PIECE: A sample, specimen, or test piece sometimes struck to test the die at various stages of development and occasionally in metals which may not be that used in actual production.

UNIFACE: Coins or medals that have designs on the obverse only, the reverse being entirely plain.

VIGNETTE: A decorative design or illustration of any kind without a definite bounding line. The picture gradually shades into the blank area of the paper. Bank notes of the nineteenth century were handsomely vignetted. The backs of our present currency also have them.

WIRE EDGE: Thin wirelike thread of metal protruding at the rim of a coin.